Download
Your
Destiny Code

How to Identify the Signals, Patterns, and Connections that Form Your Future

Dr. Mark J. Chironna

Contents

Preface

You see it all around you: a world shaken to its core. Economies, financial systems, social order, the courts, methods of communication, the nature of relationships, the role of faith—*everything* is being tested.

Even the once rock-solid American Dream seems fragile. CEOs are feeling the heat. So are their employees. Gone are the days of long-term job security. Granddad might have worked at General Electric for thirty years, but your chances of doing the same are virtually nonexistent. Instead, you will likely change jobs ten or more times before you retire, if you can retire at all. As for retiring with a pension—don't count on it. Pensions are not as common as they used to be. For many retirees, liquid assets have dwindled or evaporated altogether.

The world we once knew no longer exists. The twentieth-century sense of security enjoyed by so many has become anachronistic to the point of seeming quaint. Everything we believed to be true, everything we thought was safe is now being questioned. It is hard to reckon with all that has changed in a few short years!

Yet even in these jarring times, we can prosper. Uncertainty can be managed; deficits in hope can be restored. Tough, unfamiliar obstacles can be overcome! In our mixed-up, shook-up world, there is still enough truth to go around. Ironically, the most enduring answers to our up-to-the-minute, 21st-century dilemmas are the ones that have been tested over the course of centuries.

Uncertainty is nothing new. Shortly before he died in 1980, John Lennon wrote a song to his youngest son, Sean, who was just five years old when Lennon was killed. The prophetic lyrics spoke to the fragile side of life on planet Earth. "Before you cross the street," Lennon wrote, "take my hand, life is just what happens to you, while you're busy making other plans."[1]

The song, entitled "Beautiful Boy," was written by a man acquainted with life's inherent volatility. As a cultural icon, Lennon had run the gamut of ups and downs and knew better than most how instantaneously and irrevocably life could be changed. From his days with The Beatles, until his untimely demise, Lennon saw life's fickle side up close.

Lennon also wrote with the heart of a father determined to prepare his young son for life's inevitable surprises. The words he wrote for Sean were crafted in the certainty that life's events could not always be controlled—not by a cultural icon or a loving dad. After forty years of earthly experience, Lennon had learned that, in all its phases, life is fleeting. Just how short-lived his own life would prove to be, Lennon could not have known. Yet, even if he had lived as long as Methuselah, he most likely would have agreed that "life is like the morning fog—it's here a little while, then it's gone"[2]

The most generous lifespan passes in a cosmic microsecond. Yet the impact of a life can be felt through the millennia. That's how powerful your life can be! No matter how long or how short, your life's measure cannot be calculated in terms of time. You don't have to live as long as Methuselah to know that...

History can be made in an instant

A life can be transformed in a heartbeat

A moment of genius can turn impending disaster into unmitigated triumph.

Many memorable lives have been abbreviated. Even so, the passage of time cannot erase from our collective consciousness the likes of John Lennon; Dr. Martin Luther King, Jr.; Alexander the Great; or Amelia Earhardt. As brief as their lives were, our world still bears the imprint of their having been here. That is how jam-packed with potential we humans are! We are born with the astounding ability to press through the ceiling of time and merge with the matrix of destiny. *We are designed to accomplish extraordinary things.*

To those in the thick of difficulty and disappointment, these statements may seem out of touch with conditions on the ground. When challenges overwhelm, thoughts about big destinies seem out of place. Viewed against the backdrop of survival mode, the idea of a promising future can become abstract. It is not so surprising that we knee-jerk even our highest hopes out of sight and file them under the heading of "Pipedreams and Other Naïve Misadventures."

Does this sound like your story or, more correctly, your story up to this point? If it does, you are not alone. This book was written in part because your experience is common to people everywhere. But this book was written for another important reason: regardless of any evidence you see to the contrary, *you were created for greatness.* The power you have to define yourself is greater than the power of broken dreams to diminish you; and your power to shape your future is greater than the power of disappointment to arrest your progress.

Those who enjoy the fulfillment of their destinies would be the first to tell you how costly it is to surrender hope. Like all of us, they have known life's struggles. They have wrestled with the prospects of a dream denied. They have faced life's unexpected setbacks. Most of them entertained the idea of giving up. Yet somehow, they advanced beyond the challenges and reached the realm of reward.

Some of these dream-achievers are well-known; others live in relative obscurity. All of them have learned the secrets of living fully engaged with a sense of purpose. And all of them would concur with two statements that lie at the crux of personal destiny and therefore at the heart of this book:

1. Your ability to fulfill your purpose and potential is programmed within you, just as surely as the characteristics of your physical being are encoded in your DNA. This destiny DNA is your destiny code.
2. You can crack the code and live the life you were created to live!

Your destiny code is as unique as your fingerprint. We'll define it at length and see exactly how it functions over the course of coming chapters. For now, the point is this: becoming aware of your destiny code is your first giant step in the direction of your dreams.

As your destiny code becomes clear, the unique characteristics of your life begin to make sense. These characteristics include your abilities, the role of your relationships, even the seeming magic of life's serendipitous moments. Bit by bit, the bigger picture of your life story takes shape. You discover who you are at your very core and you know where you fit in this world. As your purpose becomes known, you begin to realize the enormity of your value as a human being.

In other words, your destiny is decoded.

Your destiny code will anchor you when seas are rough. It will keep you moving forward when the tide turns against you. With a picture of your destiny engraved in your heart, you will resist the temptation to quit or settle for less. You will be empowered to live a transformational life; you will become an agent of change and an inspiration to others.

The knowledge of your destiny code will provide the emotional, intellectual, and spiritual buoyancy needed to dispel feelings of feelings of powerlessness and encourage the belief that you are unbeatable. This is the resilience that has enabled others to achieve greatness throughout the centuries. It is this strength from within that causes you to plant your flag, maximize opportunity, and prevail in your purpose, despite the odds.

At the most fundamental level, it is the capacity to "know thyself."

Consider the story of John D. Rockefeller. Whether you dream of being a tycoon or would feel more comfortable advocating for the masses, the fact remains that Rockefeller's story tells us a lot about the workings of destiny codes.

Born into a family of six children, John's father was a traveling "pitch man,"[3] selling goods and services on the road and spending periods of time separated from his family. Back home, John's mother held down the fort and encouraged John to be enterprising. His early life reflects her influence and also reveals the unfolding of his destined path:

> By the age of 12 he had saved over $50 from working for neighbors and raising some turkeys for his mother. At the urging of his mother, he loaned a local

farmer $50 at 7% interest payable in one year. When the farmer paid him back with interest the next year Rockefeller was impressed and said of it in 1904: "The impression was gaining ground with me that it was a good thing to let the money be my servant and not make myself a slave to the money...."[4]

This revelation regarding the function of money was written into John D. Rockefeller's destiny code. At the moment he grasped the idea, the well of his life's purpose was uncapped. The picture became clearer and motivation was instilled.

Rockefeller was hardwired to accumulate money and put it to work. His purpose framed his approach to business and drove his gargantuan philanthropic efforts. What Rockefeller believed—about himself, his abilities, his role in life—created an internal system of guidance and support that sustained him through decades of endeavor.

Rockefeller was not immune to life's challenges. Like the rest of us, he had his share of bad days, including times when the focus on personal destiny was obscured. Even the inspired among us have moments of doubt when it seems that nothing short of an archaeological dig could unearth our purpose or raise our hopes from the dusty grave of disappointment.

That's where the power of a story comes in. When we are mired in the difficulties of *now*, a story can rekindle hope and remind us that we are not alone. In the unvarnished account of another human being's trials and triumphs, we can rediscover the power to press forward, grow stronger, and overcome obstacles. A story can re-energize our dreams and empower us to embrace the territory that comes with them.

When you consider the life of another human being, you realize that even "great" men and women are fallible, and many have walked in your moccasins. There is a connection between you, no matter how different that person's background, beliefs, strengths, weaknesses, heritage, or physical attributes are from your own. That kind of common bond has the tensile strength of destiny itself; it can draw you out of the morass of a tough today and pull you through the portal of tomorrow.

We will touch on several amazing stories in the pages ahead—stories of people with big dreams and small beginnings...with little hope and just enough hunger to hold on...with overwhelming challenges and the sheer nerve to overcome them.

Your reactions to these stories will be visceral. They are powerful examples—not traumatizing or revolting, but deeply moving. You will relate to youthful optimism, identify with the reality of rejection, reckon with unfair treatment, imagine the frustration, and be touched by the isolation every great man or woman has endured. But, when all is said and done, you will take hold of hope—a fresh, revitalized hope that says your dreams can be redeemed just as theirs were!

We want to believe that the great things that have happened to others can happen for us; and we *can* believe it. We are made of flesh and blood, just as they are. More importantly, we were born with as much destiny DNA as any world-changer. We have an advantage, however: we can glean from their lives and allow the light shed by their stories to bathe our own paths to glory.

The story at the heart of this book is *yours.* Wherever you are on your path at this moment, this book was written for you. Your dream may be bright, shiny, and untarnished. You may be convinced that the world is your oyster and ready to stake your claim. Or, maybe your dream has taken some heavy hits over the years. Success may seem forever out of reach. Your dream may have already cost you more than you bargained for. Maybe you never even had a dream or never believed you could reach for the stars.

Whatever your story—whether you have high hopes or feel like a dream-less wonder mired in a mud field of misfortune, you *are* a person of destiny. Whatever your spiritual persuasion or worldview, this is my invitation to embark on an adventure. Let's plumb a deep well of insight and understanding that has transformed lives. Let's position ourselves to be among those whose lives epitomize the fulfillment of potential—the immeasurable potential that can be released with every breath of life.

One way or another, the next chapter of your life will be written; I encourage you to be its author. May you find in these pages the missing pieces of your own story and a key to unlock *your* destiny—a life of untold promise and a journey like no other.

—Dr. Mark J. Chironna

Notes

1. John Lennon, "Beautiful Boy," lyrics quoted from John-Lennon.com, "Beautiful Boy," http://www.john-lennon.com/songlyrics/songs/Beautifull_Boy_Darling_Boy.htm (accessed September 26, 2008). From *Double Fantasy,* John Lennon and Yoko Ono, Geffen Records, 33 rpm, 1980.
2. James 4:14-15 (New Living Translation).
3. PBS American Experience, "The Rockefellers," http://www.pbs.org/wgbh/amex/rockefellers/peopleevents/p_rock_jsr.html (accessed September 26, 2008).
4. Ibid.

1
Chromosome Cache

*Only with winter-patience can we bring the deep
desired, long-awaited spring.*

—Anne Morrow Lindbergh

Your story is unique. The farther you tread along your destiny path, the more distinctive your life becomes. Your experiences are well-defined and singularly yours. Even so, exploring places outside of your personal experience sparks creativity and provides evidence of the inner workings of something each of us has—a destiny code.

Merriam-Webster says that *to explore* is to "…investigate, study, or analyze… to travel over (new territory) for adventure or discovery…to examine especially for diagnostic purposes…"[1] Exploration stimulates the imagination and exposes us to new perspectives. In other words, it helps us to grow. So grab your trail mix and let's explore the dynamics of a scenario from someone else's life.

Imagine that you were born the eleventh of twelve children and lived as the quintessential "golden child." Dad loved you best and there was nothing your siblings could do about it. As if your father's preferential tendencies weren't already painfully apparent to everyone, he made sure everything you had was better than everybody else's. While your siblings wore the finest Kmart had to offer, Daddy dressed you in one-of-a-kind, hand-stitched garments.

Dad meant well. He showed his undying affection with material symbols of his favor. He showered you with custom-made outfits and shiny, new toys. Everywhere your siblings turned, they saw painful reminders of the fact that no one, from the eldest to the youngest in the family, could ever capture Daddy's heart the way you had.

By the age of seventeen, you had the world on a string. Your favored position exposed you to the churning waters of your siblings' contempt. At the same time, you were protected from retaliation—as long as Daddy was nearby. From your lofty perch, you wore your couture threads proudly, unashamed of your father's love and unwilling to cast it off. You tattled when your siblings crabbed at you, adding fuel to the fire of their wrath. Your confidence in your standing was unshakable. Your deep-seated sense of security roiled family tensions. With eleven aggrieved siblings living under the same roof as you, the mounting strife could not have escaped your attention.

There was no shortage of family drama, yet you never backed away from the limelight. In fact, you outright predicted that you would lord it over the whole family one day! As you matured, you probably suspected your father of being an unfair and imperfect parent. The simmering sibling rivalry would surely have caused you to consider the possibility. But life was—well *life*. You played the hand you were dealt and lived large, assured that your future would be even brighter than your present.

Now imagine that everything changed *in an instant*. While out of Dad's protective purview, you are sold by your siblings to human traffickers, written off as dead, and subjected to searing forms of injustice. Suddenly, your big, beautiful dreams are snuffed. You are spirited away and end up far from home. No longer are you protected by your father's love. As fear of the future mounts against you, hopelessness begins to seep into the quickly darkening corners of your heart.

What would you do? How would you respond? What hope would you have to recover the life you knew? How would you ever recover what was stolen from you? Would you be able to survive the agony of betrayal? Where would you find the strength to endure the uncertainties that lay ahead? How would you summon the will to live?

Would you, in fact, have a future worth fighting for?

The answer is *yes*. That is not a flippant, Pollyanna-ish *yes*. It is an affirmation based in something that runs much deeper than unexpected catastrophes and unwelcome troubles. Even when everything good has gone bad, there is something on the inside that cannot be stolen. Deep within, your destiny code remains implanted. It wasn't lodged there by accident and it won't be shaken loose that way, either. It was planted there by your Creator and takes even stronger root as life's events unfold.

Your destiny code will be with you for the rest of your life. Each time you brush up against it, it will nudge you forward. The more destiny nudges you acknowledge, the more snapshots you will see of what is ahead. Even in a devastating moment of betrayal, as you are dragged far off course kicking and screaming, your destiny code will remind you that you that your future is worth fighting for. You are, in fact, going somewhere far beyond this trauma.

Think It Through _____

Have you ever felt as though the rug was being pulled out from under you? What was your immediate reaction? How did you get through the episode?

Your destiny code will draw you forward. It will also shed light upon past mile-markers. These signposts serve as more than reminders of glory days, disappointments, and losses. They are evidence that the unfolding of your life so far has served as critical preparation for the future. Even when your dream life turns into the ultimate nightmare, mission-readiness is being made sure. The very stresses of life are coaxing the helixes of your destiny molecules to release their instructions. As sure as the sun rises and sets, your destiny is unfolding.

When you find yourself in a miserable scenario like the one we just explored, you can discover meaning in your circumstances. If you will refuse to quit, you will realize that your life is not a cruel game of chance. The bad things that happen are not mere accidents of dysfunction; they are oddly-shaped jigsaw pieces forming the larger picture of your life—a panoramic vista that, for now, can be fully seen only in your heart and mind.

What's Good for the Goose

Every destiny is worth fighting for. *Your* destiny is worth fighting for. Downturns, reversals, and setbacks strike; yet, our lives need not end in slavery, sorrow, and suffering. There is power in a story and the story we just imagined really happened. For now, it doesn't matter when, where, or to whom. At this moment, only two things about the story must be known: First, the story turned out well—*incredibly well.* Second, luck was not a factor.

Amazing outcomes rarely happen to people who fall onto a stardust path at the precise moment that the planets line up. Real-life destiny fulfillment is no fairy tale. Neither is it a function of the universe. That is not to say that it only happens to "certain" people. Destiny fulfillment happens to everyday people who have never been assisted by fairy godmothers or wooed by princes with glass slippers. The unfolding of destiny is most often a ground-level tale of dinged-up, dust-covered dreams becoming reality, not because the dreamer is brilliant (although many are), but because the dream was identified, nurtured, and kept simmering throughout the up-and-down seasons of an imperfect life.

Great outcomes are not reserved for the world's "favorites." What's good for the goose really *is* good for the gander. If you found it difficult—even impossible—to place yourself in our story as Daddy's favorite, you still qualify for the happy ending! Having the world on a string may be as far from your life experience as the east is from the west. You may have spent your formative years on the butt-end of every-body else's dreams. It is conceivable (and not at all unlikely) that your dream was crushed even before you knew you had one.

The naked truth is that no one grew up in a perfect environment and most of us had to swim upstream from an early age. Whether you got knocked down from the top of the heap or grew up feeling like the black sheep in the family is signifi-cant because it is your life story. But there is something even more significant: your story is still unfinished. The rest of your life is waiting to be lived!

So, at some point on this side of the grave, the issue becomes: *Where will I choose to go from here?* It is a question brimming with potential. Once you agree to see the past as being *past,* the possibilities for the future become limitless. The playing field becomes level as the obstacles of the past become your platform for the future. Whether you feel like the golden child or the family's black sheep, *you decide* what comes next. There will be challenges, but you can reach your destination.

Here's the truly amazing thing: before you finish reading this book, you will discover that there is a golden child inside of you. Yes! A bigger-than-life destiny code is waiting to be unlocked. The mission, should you choose to accept it, is to expose and activate the DNA of *your* destiny.

---

des·ti·ny
noun
...A predetermined course of events often held to be an irresistible power or agency[2]

Destiny Code Defined

So, what exactly is your destiny code and how can you crack it? Let me first state the obvious: your destiny code can only be cracked if you are aware of its existence. You need to know what to look for, so read the following paragraph; it is your working definition. Then read it again, until it forms a picture in your mind:

> Your destiny code is the system of symbols, signals, and patterns that you experi-ence in your life, both in your thoughts and throughout your external circum-stances. Included in your destiny code are your relationships and the providen-tial connections that pave the way to your dreams. Your destiny code is woven into the fabric of your life and is reflected in the unique events which you have experienced. When you become aware of it, your destiny code will reveal your unique identity, purpose, and path. Your destiny code is a detailed picture of your potential.[3]

---

code

noun

...A system of signals or symbols for communication...[4]

Our working definition of *destiny code* is layered with meaning. As we explore its functions, you will see that your destiny code is not a nebulous "something out there"; it is a surprisingly concrete and accessible information source. The key is to become attuned to it and to realize that it is operating in your life right now, providing clues to your purpose and evidence of your God-given destiny.

Destiny. The word gets a lot of airplay and a significant amount of distortion in today's conversation. We tend to quantify destiny in ways that diminish our worthiness to accomplish it. Likewise, we qualify it in ways that make it seem too extraordinary to be approached by mere mortals. Most detrimental of all, we categorize it as an intangible, indefinable outcome that happens to *other* people. We inadvertently eliminate ourselves from participation and become complicit in guaranteeing that "destiny" never "happens" for us.

We need to let the hot air out of our preconceived notions. Destiny is not an ethereal concept; it is a practical one. It is as simple as this: your destiny is your identity. Let me say that again: *your destiny is your identity.* The person you were created to be is organically linked to the purpose you were created to fulfill. Therefore, your destiny code is revealed through the conduct of your life—not just the sparkling high points, but also the down-and-dirty setbacks.

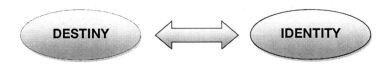

The symbols, signals, and patterns in your destiny code point to your purpose. Unless they are recognized by you and by those who play significant roles in your life, these elements will be cast off as incidents of happenstance or luck (either good or bad). Worse, they will be seen as inconsequential, as time-wasters, or as reasons to quit, often when you are at the very brink of breakthrough.

Let's assume that your middle-school music teacher took you under her wing. She offered to work with you after school; she encouraged you to audition for vocal solos; she passed on magazine articles about accomplished singers. Classmates may have been irritated by the favor you were shown. They may have voiced their envy by calling you "teacher's pet." While you appreciated the teacher's interest, you most certainly disliked the disapproval it drew from your peers.

Are these random circumstances? No. They are signals, albeit seemingly conflicting signals. On the one hand, you were favored; on the other, derided. If you (or a parent) failed to detect the significance of the circumstances, the nasty fallout might have been enough to convince you to forego your teacher's help. The price of that decision would have been far greater than mere chiding from the rest of the class.

Why? These signals reveal destiny code. A teacher with seventy singers in a single class cannot mentor each of them the way you were mentored. Your teacher signaled something important. Her actions revealed the value of your gift. She recognized a vocal quality, a musical potential that she did not see in everyone else. In time (assuming you resisted the urge to quit and withstood the backlash from your peers), you too would realize that you had something unique to offer. Your talent and the passion it engendered would reveal more of your life's purpose. Puzzle pieces would begin falling into place. One action would lead to another and then another. Followed to its ultimate conclusion, the destiny that was hinted at in middle school would play itself out on larger stages in your future!

The elements of your destiny code are diamonds in the rough. If you are looking for polished gems, you will miss these less attractive stones. They will remain buried in the unexplored depths of your life. But, if you will become an astute observer of the experiences, events, and patterns most people mistake for random occurrences, you will wield your pickax with precision to unearth the raw material of your life. You will crack the code, polish your gifts, and set in motion a continuum of accomplishment.

Recognition of your destiny code is critical. To the extent that you understand it, it will govern your mindset and guide your behavior in purposeful ways. Your destiny code will cause you to prosper by turning your observations into actions. In a very real sense, your life outcomes will be triggered by one of two things: your understanding of your destiny code or your ignorance of it.

Pack Your Bags for Destiny Fulfillment

Every one of us has experienced times of reversal. We are living in an era that has shown many people the door: careers have been upended; jobs have been lost; homes are being foreclosed; corporations are forced to the brink. It is not hard to imagine losing it all because, even if it hasn't happened to us, it has happened to people we know.

We live in a worldwide climate of uncertainty; even the ground beneath our feet seems shaky. It is a season, according to Frederic M. Hudson, in which most people feel vulnerable and susceptible rather than emergent[5] and eager to ride the next wave. Whether or not today's global instability has affected you personally, you can surely describe an event or situation that turned your world upside down. Somewhere in your past was a day that left you utterly deflated, a day that seemed to pull the plug on all hope. It might have been yesterday; it might be this moment.

If you are in the trenches of extreme adversity right now, I have a question for you. Your answer to the question (or your adjustment in response to the question) can make all the difference to your future. The question is this: *Is your dream there with you?*

During times of turmoil, we often put our dreams on the proverbial shelf, fully intending to pick them up again when the dust settles. That is precisely the knee-jerk response I mentioned in the Preface. It the reflex that kicks in, the universal default setting that is triggered when the unpleasantly unforeseen descends upon us.

There is a fallacy underlying this knee-jerk response that causes it to be more damaging than the adversity that sparked it in the first place. The misconception is that, in real life, the dust never completely settles. Disappointment and distraction are almost always in good supply. If you are waiting for the perfect time to pursue your destiny, you will wait forever.

Destiny is not fulfilled in a vacuum, it is achieved in the midst of (and even fueled by) life's circumstances.

Life is messy. Triumph implies a battle. Victories are not awarded; they are *won*. Destiny unfolds when you are waist-deep in life. It happens when you decide to dig in, dig out, and get dirty. It is as the proverb says, "Without oxen a stable stays clean, but you need a strong ox for a large harvest."[6] In a spotless stable, you don't have to wait for the dust to settle, but you won't experience any victory there, either.

Life can be *very* messy. When trial, tragedy, and trouble rear their heads, we immediately see the downside of the situation. Every danger is highlighted in neon and every pleasure seems lost for all eternity. Suddenly, we identify with Job, whose great earthly gain was turned to loss in no time flat.[7] In the midst of upheaval we feel, as Job did, that we are the most exquisitely unfortunate souls on the planet. We wonder whether we will ever enjoy being alive again.

Life often "happens" while we are "busy making other plans." When predictability is stripped away and the comfort zone shrinks or disappears altogether, we feel threatened. That is why a keen awareness of our destiny codes is so important. Difficult situations can trick us into foregoing our appointments with destiny. When today's conditions seem diametrically opposed to our dreams, we have to decide what we really believe about our lives. Do we stick by the dreams that, for now, exist only in the mind and heart? Or do we surrender those dreams to the drama playing out before our eyes?

The answer seems obvious when the question is posed for the sake of argument. It may not be as clear when the weight of the world rests upon your straining shoulders. Trials and troubles have sucked human beings into destiny derailment throughout the ages. When the circumstances scream, "Impossible!" we are easily swayed into believing the worst. While our knees begin to wobble, the temptation to surrender builds itself a head of steam.

The great danger posed by appearances of impossibility is not that we might fail. The real hazard is in our failing to perceive the opportunity that walks hand in hand with difficulty. When our lives go awry, we instinctively focus inward; we allow fear and shame about our losses to cloud our judgment; we fall prey to the belief that the mere presence of opposition is confirmation of our insufficiency. We lose sight of the fact that obstacles are a natural part of life and are, in fact, ours to overcome. When you perceive your destiny code, you understand that the trials of today can become the trophies of tomorrow!

It's time to pack your bags with your destiny code and move on. Leave behind any baggage not suited for the journey: forget about your past missteps and focus on the future. Think like a major league batter who knows that if he hits safely just once in every three at-bats, he will be a star player.

Step up to the plate that is called *today* and take your next swing!

Download Your Code

1. Describe your childhood dreams (about career, calling, achievement, marriage, etc.). Which ones are playing out in your life today? Which ones are "on the shelf"?
2. Can you identify someone whose interest in your life hinted at your destiny code? Did this person's input seem helpful, detrimental, or both? Explain.
3. How might you process this person's input differently today?
4. Can you identify a pattern of responses to life's challenges so far? Have difficulties inspired you to overcome or retreat? Refine your dream or discount it? Explain.
5. Consider what drives your mind-set; what beneficial adjustments can you make?

Notes

1. Merriam-Webster Online Dictionary 2010, s.v. "exploring," http://www. merriam-webster.com/dictionary/exploring (accessed August 17, 2010).
2. Ibid., s.v. "destiny," http://www.merriam-webster.com/dictionary/destiny (accessed August 17, 2010).
3. Dr. Mark J. Chironna, *Live Your Dream* (Shippensburg, PA: Destiny Image Publishers, 2009), 28.
4. Merriam-Webster Online Dictionary 2010, s.v. "code," http://www.merriam-webster.com/dictionary/code (accessed August 17, 2010).

5.

6. Prov. 14:4 (New Living Translation).

7. Job was a wealthy, powerful man who suffered swift and terrible tragedy, and was afterward restored to an even more favorable state (see the Bible Book of Job).

2
Uh-oh, I'm Lost

*We all face obstacles of one kind or another in life. But if you let
your deepest passion serve as your fuel, you'll be able to travel
the road back and move on to make your dreams happen.*

—Dr. Francisco Bucio

In 1985 Francisco Bucio was a medical student with a big dream—to open
a private practice in plastic surgery. As a capable resident doctor at Mexico
City's General Hospital, Bucio's dream would soon become a reality.[1] His
destiny code had been at work for years, mapping out the route to his desired
destination. The road ahead was clear; all he had to do was follow it...or so it
seemed.

On September 19, 1985, the unthinkable happened. The road to Francisco's dream was severed by a massive earthquake. Mexico City was shaken to its
core by the 8.1 trembler. Suddenly, the luxury of knowing what lay ahead was
stripped from the young man's life as tons of rubble came down in his fifth-floor
room. Bucio would be trapped for days; but it would only be a matter of moments before he realized that his ultimate surgical instrument, his right hand,
had been crushed by a steel beam.[2]

Bucio's family members were gathered at the sight when rescuers announced
the grim news: they would have to amputate the budding surgeon's hand in
order to free him from the debris. The family protested and insisted upon the
hand being saved. Rescuers did all they could to preserve the mangled hand, as
did the surgeons after them. Several weeks later, however, doctors were forced
to amputate four of Bucio's fingers. Only his thumb was left.[3] The prized right
hand of the promising surgeon-to-be was no longer functional.

11

The battle to save what remained of Bucio's hand was fierce. But the real battle was for something even more consequential: Bucio's destiny. His destiny was, after all, his identity. Francisco was created to be a plastic surgeon. Yet, five surgeries served only to keep Francisco's hand attached to his body. Imagine the feedback he must have received from well-intentioned opiners: "Francisco, you must let go of your dream and face reality. Without your hand, you are lost as a surgeon. Until you realize your new limitations, you will remain lost."

Such advice would have been understandable. By all appearances, Bucio *was* lost. He stubbornly insisted on following a path that now seemed to lead nowhere. How would he pass practical examines? How would he manage even a simple suture, no less the complex procedures involved in plastic surgery? Who in their right mind would allow a right-handed surgeon to operate on them with only one hand—his *left* hand?

Everything seemed lost...except the young man's dream. Francisco simply refused to give up. Determined to find a solution, he found a surgeon who had "pioneered the transplantation of toes to replace missing fingers."[4] Dr. Harry Buncke "replaced Francisco's ring and pinkie fingers with two of his toes."[5]

After six surgeries, Bucio achieved the unimaginable. He learned to use his oddly configured hand to perform complex tasks, including the delicate surgical procedures that were essential in his field. Imagine a plastic surgeon with two toes on his operating hand! Now imagine the founder of a major surgical center having such a hand! That is Dr. Bucio. Not only is his practice successful, but the doctor also donates his skills on behalf of those less fortunate. Dr. Francisco Bucio is living his dream.[6]

You see, destiny achievers are not immune to tribulation. They get sidetracked from time to time, just like everybody else. But deep inside, their destiny codes keep nudging them forward. These internal dream locators help destiny achievers to understand that, wherever they are in life, their purpose remains intact. They learn that being lost isn't always a mistake. Often, it is part of one's destiny code.

Fess Up to Being Lost

Francisco Bucio had to come to grips with the fact that his dream was under attack. His savaged hand surely testified to his having taken a direct hit. And, because his injury was so serious, any "normal" sense of uncertainty about future outcomes was necessarily heightened. Bucio had to have experienced moments of feeling lost.

Everyone feels lost at some point—even multiple times over the course of a lifetime. Whether those feelings always reflect reality or are triggered by shifting bouts of insecurity, "lost-ness" is a temporary condition that serves a purpose: it helps us to pinpoint our location along the destiny path. That is why being lost is a destiny code.

It is good to know that being lost is not a death sentence to your dream. Knowing this is a great start, but more information is needed to sustain consistent forward progress. Once I realize I am lost, I need to be open to a course correction. Couples often joke about the aversion many male drivers have to asking for directions. This tendency might complicate a drive in the country; but it can create real heartache in the larger scheme of destiny fulfillment.

Until you acknowledge that you are lost, you won't ask for directions. Nor will you be able to move ahead. Course corrections do more than point you in the right direction; they reset the trip clock and provide a fresh start from your current position. They are not signs of failure; they are evidence of wisdom. They reframe the journey and redeem past mistakes. Course corrections provide a new starting point and help to renew a sense of commitment to the mission of destiny fulfillment.

So what can we learn from Francisco Bucio's season of struggle? It is this: Bucio kept making adjustments and moving ahead. Like other destiny achievers, he managed to balance his emotions within the larger context of his life. As a result, his reactions did not distort the bigger picture of his dream. He continued to push forward regardless of the trauma he suffered and the uphill climb he faced. Bucio's unwillingness to quit or settle for less was not a sign of his being delusional; it was evidence of his determination to affect his future outcomes. Bucio was not a spectator; he was a man driven to take responsibility *and* his rightful place in the world.

You were not created to be a spectator. You were born to be a hands-on playmaker in the "game" of life. You are not powerless, even when the world seems to turn upside down. Whether or not you had a part in the onset of negative circumstances, you have a say in what happens next. You are free to decide what your attitude will be. Will you *feel like* a loser and even declare yourself to be one? Or will you dig deeper, find your kernel of power (your inner equip-ment to achieve a desired outcome) and turn your lemons into lemonade?

Bucio took a winning stance. His approach served him well. He chose to believe that his future was still bright, even while he recognized his human limits. Judging by his actions, it is clear that he accepted the realities of what had happened and what the implications were. He believed that success in his chosen field was still possible; but he knew that turning back the hands of time was not. The earthquake happened. It had already cost him dearly. Yet, the earthquake was not his master. Bucio still had the power to make decisions about his life that could override the effects of the earthquake.

The facts were the facts. Bucio's job was to accept them, process them, and live his dream anyway.

Acceptance and Forward Motion

You have no doubt heard the axiom: *It's not what happens that matters. It's how you respond that makes all the difference.* This is true, to a point. How you respond to adversity determines whether events will thwart you or serve your purpose in the long run. Yet, I believe that what happens *does* matter. Here's why: life's events, including the life-changing ones, are among the symbols, signals, and patterns that comprise your destiny code.

Before we continue, let's absolutely cement this important truth: there is meaning in our mountain-top experiences *and* in our setbacks. Both extremes and all the events in between contribute to our destiny development. Even our bleakest days contain opportunities for growth. The most puzzling twists and turns in our lives can take us someplace of value, if we learn to read the codes they reveal. Our life experiences are not random. Our travels—whether to the mountain tops or the valleys—lead us toward the relationships and providential connections that, over time, pave the way to our dreams.

Even the muddled days of war expose destiny codes that clarify vision and illuminate opportunity. Francisco Bucio's unimaginable trial did not subtract from his life; it added new facets of understanding to his life's mission. Having endured the pain of multiple procedures and confronted the fear of loss and even further mutilation, Bucio developed a deeper appreciation for the fears that plagued his surgical patients.[7] They no doubt sensed his genuine compassion and found comfort in it.

Acceptance of what has already happened is foundational to future development, as is the realization that destiny is not achieved without the help of others. Crises awaken us to the fact that the lone-ranger approach is unsustainable. We *need* other people in our lives. The pressures of profound circumstances help us to shed the stubborn self-sufficiency we work so hard to protect.

With his life's mission on the line, Bucio could not afford to withdraw from others. To wallow in self-pity or wander into isolation would be to separate himself from available solutions and resources. Instead of retreating to lick his wounds, Bucio mounted a frontal assault on his injuries. He dug in, reached out, and found people who were uniquely positioned to help him.

Dr. Harry Buncke was one of those people—a providential connection who would help Bucio achieve his goals. The combination of Bucio's determination and Buncke's surgical genuis produced an unusual solution: two of Bucio's missing fingers would be replaced with toes! It wasn't the solution Bucio envisioned during his four days under the earthquake rubble. It was, however, the answer he needed to have a functional right hand and a private surgical practice!

Other people helped to bring Bucio's destiny to pass. Some helped with his rehabilitation; others contributed to his continued education at the hospital.[8] One surgeon-in-training created an opportunity that proved to be pivotal in Bucio's life:

> A senior resident had been watching Francisco progress from cleaning and wrapping wounds to executing simple surgical procedures like removing moles. He asked Francisco to assist in an operation on a man with a broken nose. The procedure was extremely delicate, and Francisco assumed he would simply pass the instruments. But as the resident prepared to remove cartilage from the man's rib for use in rebuilding the nose, he turned to Francisco and said, "You get the cartilage."

It was Francisco's moment of truth, and he knew it.[9]

After all he had been through, Bucio remained present to the moment. From the very onset of his post-earthquake journey, he kept his sights set on success. To keep the dream alive in his heart, he must have imagined a variety of scenarios that could lead to the resurgence of his dream. All he needed was a chance to prove himself. When his moment came, Bucio knew full well what was riding on it. He had waited for his chance, and when it arrived, he made the most of it.

Such clarity can only exist in the presence of true acceptance. By accepting the past, we position ourselves to embrace new ideas and methods for destiny fulfillment. If we place the past, however thorny it might be, it in the context of our life's purpose, we can make it work for us, even when it exacts a heavy price in the short term. How do we do this? Through vigilance; we must remain alert to the day-by-day, moment-by-moment revelation of our destiny codes—and ready to act upon them.

Accept the fact that you cannot change the past, and you will be free to choose the future your destiny code reveals.

Freedom in Acceptance

Do you see how acceptance creates freedom? Can you think of an existing situation that would be transformed by such liberty? Have you reached an impasse in some area of your life? Is there a deadlock that you cannot seem to break? Could it be that you have been holding out, hoping that the facts on the ground will change in ways that make them more palatable? Are you frozen in place waiting for the perfect moment to act?

Let's turn Bucio's story around for a moment to see how easily he might have forfeited freedom and subjected himself to a stalemate. Bucio might have insisted on a particular outcome; he might have been guided by the emotional need to have a "normal-looking" right hand.

So, what if he had refused Dr. Buncke's offer to reconstruct his hand with the mix-and-match digits Bucio ended up having? His refusal would have not have been surprising, under the circumstances. He might easily have said: "I am studying to be a *surgeon*. The earthquake was not *my* plan. There's only one way for me to continue on my career path: I need a right hand with five fingers and *no* toes. Period."

Such a stance would have seemed logical, but would have proved impractical, especially in 1985. Bucio might have searched the world over and never found a way to make his dream come true in the precise way he preferred. The long-term cost could easily have been greater than the short-term price of acceptance. While he searched for the perfect solution, Bucio's career as a plastic surgeon might have been placed on indefinite hold. Over time, any number of factors—a new family, financial depletion, or discouragement—could have made returning to school more difficult. With challenges piling higher, the temptation to quit would arguably have become more attractive.

Had Bucio not accepted his situation and options at face value, the perfect would have become the enemy of the good. He might have ended up with a nicer-looking hand, but it might have come at the expense of his larger destiny. Thankfully, Bucio had the intestinal fortitude to process disappointment and make the adjustments necessary to continue his forward momentum. He maintained the freedom to make beneficial choices. In turn, his choices created the space needed for circumstances to shift in favor of his destiny fulfillment, even when fulfillment seemed excruciatingly incremental.

In retrospect, it is clear that Bucio's freedom to choose generated long-term benefits: He became a prominent plastic surgeon, thereby fulfilling his dream. He became a highly productive member of society. He is able to help others in need of his services, including those who are unable to afford surgery.

Becoming "lost" (being thrown off your expected pathway to destiny and into an unfamiliar set of circumstances) can happen in an instant. Acceptance may take more time. There is a process involved with your freedom to choose. The trial itself provides that process.

Trial   Process

When unforeseen circumstances arise, new choices present themselves. When these previously unconsidered options pop up, the ball drops in our court—but it is a bigger court than before. The number of available plays has increased. Our thinking, which was centered on a limited number of perceived choices, must become more elastic to embrace the expanded playbook. Decisions will have to be made. They will in fact be made even if we fail to act, because doing nothing is a decision, too.

The process of exploring your freedom to choose isn't always easy, but it always produces movement. This freedom is often discovered when we feel lost. Remember, being lost is an element of your destiny code. It will prompt you to ask for direction. It will soften your resistance to needing and receiving help.

We can do this. To live fully, we *must*.

Matched With Mentors

With acceptance under your belt, it is easier to allow people—the right people—to come alongside and encourage you on your destiny path. Whether they mentor you formally or not, these encouragers are mentors. A mentor might be someone with expertise in your field of endeavor. It can also be someone who simply points you in the right direction in some area of your life. In either case, mentors will help you recognize your destiny code and, therefore, your identity.

Mentors recognize potential and have a passion to see it realized. A mentor can help identify misperceptions and blind spots in your thinking. A good mentor can help you to shatter false expectations and build the healthy expectations that promote excellence. Mentors meet you at pivotal points along your destiny path and help you to find the next piece of the puzzle. They help to unlock your potential, often by exposing new horizons or new facets of existing opportunity that you might otherwise screen out due to misperceptions about your identity or abilities.

Think It Through _____

Do you have someone in your life who can help you unlock your potential? Are you open to a mentor's input?

Mentors are rarely the people you thought they would be. They are the very people your assumptions often obscure from view. This is precisely the benefit they offer: they add value by presenting perspectives that might not otherwise occur to you. Their experiences enable them to shed light and promote personal growth. Because your mentors are passionate about the fulfillment of your destiny, they are willing to be direct. They will help you cut away the slack in your thinking or methods. They will urge you to raise the bar in matters of character, creativity, and achievement. Mentors will speak to your head *and* your heart.

A good mentor will help pull you through the lost places by refining your focus and identifying what is needed for you to advance. Whether your mentor is a PhD or an eighth-grade dropout, he or she will possess the kind of wisdom and stature that will command your attention. More often than not, a mentor will speak into your life, not by telling you things, but by asking key questions.

When you are lost, a mentor can help to define your location by asking, "What are you looking for?" This simple question can trigger a heightened focus and a renewed appreciation of the destiny connections already evident in your life. How you respond to your mentors and other destiny connections will determine how much value you will derive from their input and how far you will venture into newly-recognized fields of opportunity.

The resident surgeon who invited Francisco Bucio to perform a delicate surgical procedure was a mentor, even if only for a moment. He saw Bucio's potential; he had a heart for Bucio's destiny; he pulled Bucio out of a season of limbo. Bucio expected to do nothing more that day than to pass the instruments. But in much the same way as Dr. Buncke reattached digits to Bucio's ruined hand, the resident gave Bucio the means to reattach his gifting to his dream.

It was a turning point on Bucio's destiny road. He knew it; so did his mentor. Each responded to the moment with a level of seriousness and clarity that reopened realms of possibility. Bucio acted on all that had germinated in his heart over the course of his lifetime. He seized the moment; but it was his mentor who unlocked it.

The Power of Taking Responsibility

Notice that when the unexpected moment of opportunity arose, Bucio was prepared and deliberate in his response. He had already groomed himself to emerge from the "lost" state to the "next" place of development and opportunity.

Bucio's condition of readiness was not accidental. Nor did it result solely from the opportunity offered by the resident surgeon. Bucio had carefully set the stage for opportunity to be met by preparation. Throughout his post-earthquake journey, he had taken responsibility for his outcomes. His story demonstrates the profound power of taking responsibility. This power is released in and through our lives when we refuse to be confined to the emotional prison of victimhood.

If we accept it, a victim mentality will keep us virtually paralyzed. Bucio refused this outcome. Never passive and always moving forward, he swallowed his share of disappointment and found a way to convert it into indomitability. He was willing to endure the quizzical looks of others. Having no hard proof that his choices and actions would lead to success, he was willing to give it his best effort. He would risk even failure in exchange for a shot at his dream.

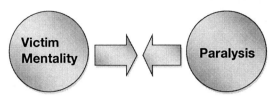

As golden as it was, the opportunity given him in the surgical theatre would have amounted to nothing had Bucio not been prepared to capitalize on it. Had he not accepted the past, received the help of others, and submitted himself to a relentless regimen of rehabilitation, his new "fingers" would have been little more than appendages filling up the space beyond his knuckles.

Bucio made courageous choices and pushed the boundaries of what seemed possible. He held out hope for the saving of his own fingers until it was clear that amputation was unavoidable, but he never stopped seeking solutions, even after his fingers were lost. As a result, he found the right people to support his cause. Bucio's choices paid off, not only for his life, but for the life of every patient he has been able to serve.

When the chips are down and all seems lost, you can choose to be proactive. If you have been prone to passivity thus far, don't wait for an earthquake to shake you out of the doldrums. Begin to develop a healthy sense of responsibility little by little. Start by making relatively small choices—about diet, health, work habits—and allow that training to prepare you for the big decisions that will inevitably come your way. Imagine how far ahead of the game you will be if you take responsibility for your role *before* a crisis strikes.

Taking responsibility is a form of acceptance. When we take our place at the table of life, we embrace the understanding that we have influence over our circumstances and our world. We acknowledge and empower ourselves to act upon the truth that we were built to overcome life's challenges. As responsible people (and not victims), we will more readily identify and value our unique gifts, and step onto the paths to our individual destinies!

Beware the Dream-killers

You are aware of the important role played by mentors. If you have walked the earth for any length of time, you are also aware that not everyone in your life brings a positive influence to the party.

At any given moment, there are two kinds of human influencers in our midst: mentors and dream-killers. Mentors lift us up and help us to set our sights higher. Dream-killers do quite the opposite; they are the naysayers who climb out of the woodwork the moment you begin your destiny pursuit in earnest. Oddly enough, dream-killers are the first ones to recognize your gift; but instead of encouraging its development, they try to kill it before it matures.

Dream-killers are not required by law to wear caution labels warning of their toxicity. Some of them don't even realize, on a conscious level, that their words and actions are destructive. Often, they fly under the radar and become your best friends. You might spend years and even decades daydreaming with them. The two of you might have sat countless times over latte and biscotti swapping hopeful stories of future victories. Yes, these two-legged "wet blankets" often seem to be on board with our big dreams—until they see signs that those dreams are about to be lived in the here and now.

That is when the dream-killing gene is activated and your trusted confidante reveals his or her insecurity. Suddenly, instead of cheering you on, your two-legged wet blanket becomes an uninvited cynic whose mission is to question your dream, diminish your abilities, and dump a dose of so-called reality into the realm of possibility that surrounds you. When this shift occurs, your relationship will fracture into two distinct territories. One is the safe ground of superficiality. There, you can talk about the weather, the color of your new sofa, and the name of your hairstylist.

The other territory—the place of significance—is protected by a fierce guard dog and a prominent "Do Not Enter" sign. If you venture past this emotional checkpoint, you will meet with some unexpected resistance. Any good news you share is likely to be met with a heaping spoonful of passive-aggression and a well-placed "Oh, really?"

Dream-killing is a fear-based activity involving feelings and acts of jealousy aimed at those who seem to be pulling ahead of the pack. Remember, anyone can choose destiny-achievement, including the dream-killers among us. But those who seek to burst your bubble prove by their cynicism that they have already disqualified themselves from the prize you continue to seek.

Something real or imagined is standing between the dream-killer and his or her dream. It may be an insecurity, misperception, or perceived handicap; chances are that it is a barrier existing only in the mind and heart. It is the reason why only a small percentage of people fully commit to their life's purposes and even fewer see their decisions through to completion. As a result, the supply of naysayers is virtually limitless.

Relationships with committed dream-killers require wisdom. If left unchallenged, the toxicity sown by jealousy can permeate the entire relationship. Unless you handle such a relationship proactively, you could be lulled into sacrificing your destiny on the altar of friendship. However, if you take a stand, your resident dream-killer just might get over his or her fear of being left behind. With a little tough love and a lot of understanding, the insecurities that fuel dream-defying cynicism can be healed. Your former dream-killer can become an ardent supporter. Sadly, this outcome is not always possible to achieve.

Bear in mind that not all dream-killers are friends or co-workers. Some are your loved ones. I am not recommending that you disown family members. You will, however, need to find positive ways to establish healthy boundaries within which their attempts to chip away at your destiny commitment are neutralized. No one can kill your dream without your permission.

Don't get angry at the wet blankets in your life; love them the best you can and continue to live your life to the fullest.

Your Inherent Value

Standing up to dream-killers is always easier when you know who you are. This knowledge must extend beyond the generalization that every human being is precious. Every person *is* precious; but knowing who you are means taking that truth a step further. You must be convinced that *your* inherent value is beyond measure!

If dream-killers are having their way with you, it is time to check your belief systems about *self*. Do you believe that your dream is worthwhile? Even more importantly, do you believe you are worthy of achieving it? Do you see the fulfillment of your destiny as an outgrowth of your being? Is it based in a firm conviction about your purpose in life? Or has achievement become a salve for low self-esteem, a performance-mentality mechanism designed to help you feel better about yourself?

Everyone, at one time or another, deals with issues of diminished self-worth. Often, these issues arise after actual or perceived failures. When a project, relationship, or career fails, we tend to ascribe the negative outcome to some flaw embedded in us. For example, when companies are forced to downsize, those who lose their jobs frequently struggle with questions of their own worthiness. In reality, the downsizing was nothing personal; yet, if we base our value on some aspect of performance, we will assign layoffs to the category of "Personal Failures."

Most often, this kind of reaction stems from self-worth issues that began earlier in life. Many factors of upbringing and other childhood experiences can leave their mark on our perceptions of self. Often, they leave emotional scars that linger for years and even lifetimes. Whatever the source of our doubts regarding self-worth, they leave us more vulnerable to attacks against our sense of personal destiny. This is true in part because diminished self-worth elevates natural fears of rejection. When these fears drive our behavior, we work hard to please others—sometimes going so far as to forfeit our God-given dreams in order to remain in the good graces of those we love.

Let me briefly address self-worth with a passage from my book, *Live Your Dream*:

> My desire…as a life coach, is for you to become an unabashed proponent of your destiny—a man, woman, or youth convinced of the truth that you are fearfully and wonderfully made and designed with boundless potential….The very fact of your birth is irrefutable evidence of your significance. Your inherent value as a person exceeds that of any other creature or created thing. Untold worth resides within you; therefore, the outcomes of your life are consequential….[10]

You cannot earn self-worth; you are born with it. Our value comes not from our *doing,* but from our *being.* (In this case, *being* refers not to the physical body, but the fact of existence.)

Seasons Come; Seasons Go

A quick word about life's seasons. (For in-depth coverage of this topic, see my book, *Live Your Dream*). Our lives are dynamic. At any given moment, multiple factors are in play. These factors shift and evolve over time. Some factors operate through the duration of our lives. Some of these are called *unique factors,* a term we will discuss in greater depth later on.

For now, let's assume that you are a gifted entrepreneur. Your ability in this area has shown up in a variety of ways throughout your lifetime. It affects your passions, pursuits, and even your habits. It may play a role in your professional life. Although your gift may be more or less active at certain times, it can never be deleted from your makeup as a human being. If you were an entrepreneurial teen, you will likely show a similar resourcefulness in later years. Your entrepreneurial spirit is part of who you are.

Age, appearance, and certain activities change over the years. You can't have the supple skin of a teen forever and you won't play in the NFL when you are seventy-nine. If you are a parent, parenthood will always be part of your identity. You will enjoy having little ones underfoot for a season, but you won't always have baby-gates guarding the stairways in your home.

The changing of seasons is not only healthy, it is necessary for growth. Changing seasons help to keep us alert and attuned to our progress. Seasonal shifts help us to focus on "now" endeavors; they help us to develop new routines in support of meaningful pursuits. When the seasons change, they signal shifts in momentum and even direction. I might weed my garden daily during springtime and summer, but in the winter months, I will apply that energy to snow removal and the stacking of wood for the fireplace.

No two seasons are alike, yet each season serves a specific purpose in the unfolding of destiny. Some seasons are more enjoyable than others; some are downright taxing. To stay on the destiny path, we need to find ways to weather all kinds of seasons. Our destiny codes help us to achieve that kind of balance. With a strong sense of your destiny code in mind, you will be better able to appreciate the benefit of spring rains. You will remain content when January snows make a trip to the mailbox challenging. When you accept the fact that every season has a reason, you will be able to handle all kinds of "weather."

Whether you are the butcher, baker, candlestick maker, or President of the United States, you destiny will unfold over the course of many seasons. Each will present its own challenges and rewards and each will produce additional evidence of your destiny code. As seasons change, you will discover fresh fields of opportunity and new ways to fulfill your purpose.

Location, Location, Location

When was the last time you said, "Uh-oh, I'm lost"? Was it five years ago…or five minutes ago? Do the realities of your circumstances, when compared with your expectations, cause you to feel lost even now? Do you feel like you are chasing your tail and being yanked back by the leash of the "urgent"? Are the important pursuits of destiny fulfillment lying dormant like bones buried long ago beyond the reach of your current chain?

Don't be afraid to 'fess up! Being lost is a destiny code. The point of this book is not to paint a primrose path; it is to uncover your destiny codes and create the space—the permission, in a sense—for you to understand those codes and act upon them. Being lost is not always a mistake. It is a location. It is the reset point for the rest of your life, the current step on your destiny path. What you learn here will serve your purpose in the months and years to come.

What you learn in the lost place, and the people you meet here, are among the missing pieces you have been seeking. Whether you realized it or not, you needed to get here—the lost place—in order to reach the "found" places your dream is designed to take you.

Download Your Code

1. Which part of Francisco Bucio's story speaks most directly to your own? Explain why and describe how you can apply lessons from that part of his story (and any other part) to your life today.
2. Write down the names of any dream-killers in your life. What specific steps can you take to neutralize them?
3. What adjustments can you make in the area of accepting your past and correctly assessing your inherent self-worth? How might the resulting freedom show up in your life? Be specific.

4. What adjustments can you make in the area of accepting your need for other people to be part of your destiny path? In what ways might have you have hindered those relationships from having their full effect in the past?
5. How would you characterize your current season? What features of it do you like? Which features cause discomfort or consternation? What is this season producing in terms of learning and destiny development?

Notes

1. Cynthia Kersey, *Unstoppable; 45 Powerful Stories of Perseverance and Triumph from People Just Like You* (Naperville, IL: Sourcebooks, Inc., 1998), 59.
2. Ibid.
3. Ibid., 60.
4. Ibid.
5. Ibid., 61.
6. Ibid., 61-62.
7. Ibid., 62.
8. Ibid., 61-62.
9. Ibid.
10. Dr. Mark J. Chironna, *Live Your Dream: Planning for Success,* (Shippensburg, PA: Destiny Image Publishers, 2009), 19.

3
Next Stop…Where?

There is no security on this earth, there is only opportunity.

—General Douglas MacArthur

Security. It is often treated as life's most precious commodity. Yet, those who enter destiny's halls know how quickly the focus on security can blind us to one of life's highest pursuits: the fulfillment of purpose.

There is no question that security, as fleeting and unreliable as it is, feels good for as long as it sticks around. When you feel secure, you feel comfortable. The sense of security makes it easy to curl up on the couch with a good book and indulge the perks of everyday life. The fact is that security in this natural realm is, above all else, a feeling that is subject to conditions on the ground. It appears, disappears, and reappears often.

Security cannot be guaranteed or made permanent. Even when we think we have apprehended it, we quickly discover that it is a moving target. If you are destitute, a few dollars in pocket brings a taste of security; it might provide a much-needed meal or something to drink. But a meal cannot satisfy forever, and insecurity inevitably returns.

For those who have accumulated wealth, there is a sense of having arrived at the place of being secure. The bills are paid, desires can be indulged, and unexpected needs can be met. But a new threat emerges: the fear of losing what you have gained over time. The security level must be raised to protect everything of value. Yet, not even the wealthy can ensure 100 percent safety for their assets or their loved ones.

The desire for security is a relentless taskmaster. It is elusive and deceiving. It strokes the part of the psyche that desires control and self-protection. It entices us to park in the *now* and preserve the safety that has visited us. As a goal, the search for security assures future disappointment. Sooner or later, your planned "program" will be yanked without notice. Often, this bodes well for destiny fulfillment, because the ethereal sense of being secure beckons us to wrap ourselves in *what is* and postpone attending to *what could be.*

Security has its benefits in protecting life and limb. It protects *against* change and is a good manager of the status quo. By definition, there are certain things it cannot do. It cannot urge you forward. It does not inspire you to win; it is a defensive tool designed to find ways not to lose. Security will not guide you over obstacles; it will show you how to avoid them. Security will make you safer, but it cannot and will not make you stronger. Nor will it help you to define your destiny path. Security can produce feel-good sensations, but its overemphasis guarantees stunted growth.

Advancement toward the fulfillment of your purpose falls under the purview of security's nemesis—the "lost" place where we are confronted by the unknown. When we are unsure of where we are and even less sure of where we are headed, we are primed to learn the most about who we are, why we are here, and how much we are designed to accomplish.

Rude Awakenings

You *need* to make a stop in the lost place in order to reach the "found" places your dream is designed to take you. The state of being lost is really a state of being headed someplace unfamiliar. It is a destiny Rototiller that breaks up the smooth, hard soil of your life and exposes new, unexpected paths of opportunity—often at what seem to be the most inopportune times. You might not feel secure in these situations, but if you remain open to them, you will discover opportunities for destiny fulfillment that could never be revealed in the comfort zone.

One of the most outstanding stories of "lost-ness" and destiny fulfillment I have ever encountered—the story of the "golden child" mentioned in Chapter 1— illustrates this truth better than almost any biography I know. It is the story of Joseph, a figure well-known to Jews, Muslims, and Christians, but relevant to people from all persuasions and walks of life. Joseph's experiences with rejection, betrayal, abandonment, and ultimately, promotion of the highest order, capture the imaginations of all who have experienced pain and desire another crack at living the lives of their dreams.[1] A brief walk in Joseph's life story is about to yield important secrets about the dynamics and promise of *your* destiny code.

As you recall, Joseph was the eleventh of twelve children. He enjoyed the good life and looked forward to a terrific future. Two dreams convinced him that his destiny road would be extraordinary. In his first dream, the brothers' sheaves of grain bowed down to Joseph's sheaves. In the second dream, the sun, moon, and eleven stars bowed down to Joseph. These dreams revealed to young Joseph a future of great favor in which he would rise in stature above his family and even the cosmos as he knew it.[2]

Naïve and precocious, Joseph shared his dreams with his father and brothers, stoking the fires of jealousy and feeding a seething rage that would change all of their lives forever. Infuriated at the insinuation that their little brother would even presume to lord it over them, the brothers were motivated to do all they could to ensure the impossibility of such an outcome.

They committed an act so crushing to Joseph's presumed destiny as to seem final. They sold him to slave traders and led their father, Jacob, to believe that he had been mauled to death by a wild animal. As Jacob grieved for his lost son, Joseph was shipped to Egypt and sold into slavery. There he would serve in the home of an Egyptian captain named Potiphar.

In the blink of an eye, Joseph had been toppled from his pedestal of favor and cast into the pit of utter impossibility. The dreams of the aspiring young leader were suspended indefinitely. Joseph's familiar life and expected destiny path had been interrupted at best, severed at worst. For all intents and purposes, his dream was dead on arrival in Egypt.

In reality, Joseph's rise to the top had begun in earnest.

Would You Repeat That?

Imagine the questions racing through Joseph's mind in the frantic moments of his betrayal and enslavement: "Why are you doing this? How could you do this? I am your brother! Don't you love me—at all? How will I get home? When will I see my father again? Where are these men taking me?"

Burly traders reply, "Settle down, boy. Your next stop is Egypt."

The teenager pleads, "My next stop is *where?*"

Joseph's world was completely upended. Can you relate to such a quagmire? Although it is unlikely that you have experienced the horrors of being sold into human trafficking, you have almost certainly asked the same plaintive question Joseph did: "My next stop is *where?* Would you mind repeating that?"

You may have cried out in fear and despair when your retirement fund evaporated the year before you turned sixty-five. You may have wept and wondered *why* after the tragic loss of a child. Perhaps you received a received a diagnosis that stopped the clock and arrested your dreams of tomorrow. Maybe you lost the home you spent half your lifetime paying off. There is not a soul on Planet Earth who hasn't felt completely lost and headed in the wrong direction after an unforeseen event, tragedy, or act of betrayal. This sense of being cast adrift is many-faceted and often delivers the following realizations:

A familiar landscape is significantly altered or replaced with an unfamiliar setting.

A longstanding belief or belief system is shaken so that ideas about what is fact and what is fiction must be reevaluated.

That which was considered trustworthy is proven to be unreliable.

Support systems are compromised or disappear altogether.

Routines are disrupted or entirely rearranged.

When unforeseen, unwanted, and traumatic changes occur, we feel betrayed (by people or by the facts as we saw them); we feel alone (having to relate in new ways to new people under new conditions of uncertainty); we feel forced out of safety (yanked from the comfortable zones we have carved out for ourselves); we feel vulnerable (tossed by turbulence over which we seem to have no control).

Surely Joseph experienced all of these emotions. It is what he did with them that really matters. But before we examine his handling of the unexpected, let's explore a powerful twenty-first century story of a victory that was wrestled from the jaws of defeat.

Managing Thought Momentum

Have you ever been in a wreck or a near miss and watched your life pass before your eyes? Traumatic moments ratchet up our thought processes. Ideas and images race across the silver screen of the mind at an impossible rate of speed. This frenetic level of mental activity is an extreme but finite example of thought momentum.

In our waking moments, our thought-life is under our control. Even in the adrenalin-filled moments during a wreck or other mishap, we *can* choose our thoughts. We can choose to surrender in fear and allow disaster or death to overtake us. Or we can focus on finding split-second solutions that can change what seems to be an inevitable outcome.

Captain Chelsey "Sully" Sullenberger knows something about operating under that kind of pressure. As a pilot for U.S. Airways, he is accustomed to the rigors of jet flight and suited to the demands of the profession. On what seemed to be an ordinary January day, Sullenberger commanded a five-minute flight that would become one of the most well known in aviation history.

On January 15, 2009, the Airbus A320 under Sully's command was scheduled to carry 155 souls from New York City to Charlotte, North Carolina.[3] Flight 1549 took off from LaGuardia Airport and began its ascent. No doubt, people on board read magazines, dozed, or prepared for meetings. Everyone on the aircraft had plans pertaining to their arrival in Charlotte. They knew where they were going and they expected to reach their common destination at a specific time.

In a heartbeat, everything changed. Within three minutes of takeoff, the plane collided with a flock of geese. The cabin filled with the odor of something burning as the large birds were sucked into the now incapacitated engines. Almost instantly, the engines' high-decibel whirring wound down to a whisper. A bird strike had turned a high-tech airliner into an airborne deathtrap—and the teeming streets and towers of New York City lay vulnerable below.

Captain Sully was in an untenable position. One way or another, his aircraft was going down. The seasoned pilot had to use what few resources remained within his control to bring about the best possible outcome in what was shaping up to be a worst-case scenario.

Sullenberger rose to the occasion. He summoned his greatest natural asset: his ability to think. In order to gain control of the hobbled aircraft, he had to first rein in his thoughts. Imagine the momentum of adrenalin-laced images and ideas that careened through his mind! Not only would his own life have passed before his eyes, but the lives of scores and possibly hundreds of people hung in the balance.

The captain quickly corralled his thoughts, sorted and prioritized them, and used them to formulate a plan of action. He determined that his chances of safely returning the aircraft to LaGuardia were virtually nonexistent. If such an attempt failed, the Airbus would likely crash on busy city streets. It would be a catastrophe of enormous proportions. Continuing west and landing in New Jersey wasn't an option either.

There was just one place left to put down the aircraft: *the Hudson River.*

Handling the disabled aircraft as a megaton glider, Sullenberger threaded the needle between the near banks of the Hudson River—Manhattan on one side and New Jersey on the other. Passengers had already dropped their magazines and realized that Charlotte, North Carolina was no longer a viable destination. As the plane glided south along the river and its frigid surface drew closer, the pilot calmly said, "Brace for impact."[4]

Imagine the passengers' question: "We're landing *where?*"

Captain Sullenberger brought the jetliner to rest and comparative safety on the river's icy waters. With no life lost and an incalculable tragedy averted, a "previously unknown fifty-seven-year-old pilot, Chelsey B. Sullenberger, became an overnight hero…."[5]

Sully's heroism had not developed overnight. He was one of the best in his field and a man more prepared for a landing on the Hudson than almost anyone else. He had spent four decades preparing for this pivotal point on his destiny path. Even so, Sully needed more than technical expertise to manage Flight

1549's drift into uncharted aviation territory. Sullenberger had to take command over his mind and manage the thought momentum that would make "The Miracle on the Hudson" possible.

Chelsey Sullenberger used his mind perfectly and drew upon his entire life history—the outward signs of his destiny code—to fulfill his purpose that day. His own words say it best:

> In many ways, all my mentors, heroes, and loved ones—those who taught me and encouraged me and saw the possibilities in me—were with me in the cockpit of Flight 1549. We had lost both engines. It was a dire situation, but there were lessons people had instilled in me that served me well.…
>
> I've done a lot of thinking since then about all the special people who mattered to me, about the hundreds of books on flying that I've studied, about the tragedies I've witnessed again and again as a military pilot, about the adventures and setbacks in my airline career, about the romance of flying, and about the long-ago memories.
>
> I've come to realize that my journey to the Hudson River didn't begin at LaGuardia Airport. It began decades before, in Mr. Cook's grass airfield, in the skies over North Texas, in the California home I now share with my wife, Lorrie, and our two daughters, and on all the jets I've flown toward the horizon.
>
> Flight 1549 wasn't just a five-minute journey. My entire life led me safely to that river.[6]

Your entire life will lead you forward into *your* destiny. However, you cannot glide there safely without being prepared and vigilant to direct your thoughts in a beneficial way. Throughout your life, as you hone your gifts, talents, and skills, thought momentum is a constant. It is always building in one direction or another.

The question is, are your thoughts building in a positive direction or a negative one?

Oppose Opposing Voices

The challenges Chelsely Sullenberger faced were different from those faced by Joseph. Yet both men found themselves unexpectedly heading into the realm of the unknown, where new questions arise with every passing second and voices scream of the impossibilities ahead. Neither man could accurately predict the outcome of their trial, but each man had to make quick decisions as to how to conduct themselves in the worst possible conditions.

No doubt, a raging stream of fearful thoughts competed for Joseph's attention on the fateful day when his brothers conspired so brutally against him. He probably feared for his life and dreaded whatever other atrocities were ahead. It is likely that he considered methods of escape. He probably racked his brain for any possible way to reverse the awful trajectory upon which he had been thrust.

The precise momentum of Joseph's thoughts is unrecorded, but we can take the information we have and consider it in light of what we know about human nature. We know that an unbridled momentum of negative thoughts typically leads to a state of emotional (and even physical) paralysis. When we consciously or unconsciously surrender to a belief in inevitable doom, we dilute our personal power to solve problems, escape danger, or survive a downturn.

Conversely, the very fear of capture and the threat of increasing danger can be used to inspire monumental acts of resistance. You have probably heard stories of parents who lifted automobiles in order to free their trapped, injured children. This is partly a physical phenomenon based on an adrenalin surge. But there is a mental component, too. That component is *choice*. Faced with such a crisis, it would be easy to allow myself to fall to pieces at the sight of my injured child. Staying in control of my thoughts and becoming part of the solution takes a little more work. Whatever I choose, thought momentum is building and will contribute to the outcome of the crisis.

Even while missing some of the details of Joseph's journey, we know that he "pulled a Sullenberger." The situation he faced seemed beyond all reach of hope. The change in his "flight path" led him in the exact opposite direction of his expected destination. Yet we know that Joseph pulled victory out of the jaws of defeat, just as Sully did. He managed the opposing voices in his head. He took command over his circumstances and fulfilled his destiny in ways that no one could have imagined.

Think of the pivotal moments in your life when opportunity knocked. Where did your thoughts take you? If you are like most people, you heard positive and negative "voices" virtually simultaneously. Your inner dialogue may have gone something like this:

"Finally! My ship has come in! This is the ticket to my dream."

Just as your hopes began to rise, an opposing voice chimed in. "I've been down this road before. Each time something good happened, the going eventually got tough and I quit. This success won't last any more than it has in the past."

The opposing voices you heard attested to the things you believed at some level. You *believed* that a golden opportunity had been presented; but you did not fully believe that you were up to the task. Part of you got in the game and part of you hedged. Still, the final outcome remained in your hands.

Think It Through _____

What opportunity is before you? Are you more likely to seize it with confidence or withdraw from it because of self-doubt? What do you stand to gain or lose?

Remember: it was what Joseph *did* with his thoughts that mattered in the end. So it was for Chelsey Sullenberger. He surely considered the possibility of a bad ending. He had to consider a variety of outcomes in order to make a wise choice. But the final outcome of his ordeal was determined in large part by what he *did* with the opposing voices in his head.

Sullenberger set aside the thoughts that interfered with a positive outcome and focused on finding solutions. He chose to behave his way into his future. He governed his thoughts, made careful decisions (in a very limited time span), and acted on those decisions.

You will never eliminate opposing voices completely, but you can master them.

Your Dream at Work

Not all crises are resolved in a day. Joseph's situation played out over the course of years. As already mentioned, he fulfilled a grand destiny before his life was over.

We all know modern-day stories of people rose above dire and even overwhelming circumstances to live highly fulfilling, productive lives. Helen Keller, Stephen Hawkings, Abraham Lincoln, George Washington come to mind. All of these individuals were driven from within to overcome the circumstances and pursue their destinies despite the unbelievable odds stacked against them.

What keeps people like these folks going when disability, chronic illness, national crises, and the logistics of battle seem to be working against them? I believe it is their awareness of their destiny codes and their unflinching cooperation with their unfolding destinies.

With a dream in your heart and a belief that the events of your life are meaningful, you will find a way to press forward. A sense of purpose affects your psyche and everything that issues from it. Your dream touches your imagination, giving you clear vision to move forward. Your dream touches your perceptions, giving you the ability to filter out opposing voices and any thoughts, choices, or actions that run counter to your dream.

Your dream, as revealed by and in your destiny code, impacts your will by aligning your worldview, your priorities, your emotions, and the rationing of your energy. Provided your dream is built on the foundation of your God-given destiny code and not a misguided desire for fame or fortune, it will serve to undergird your life's purpose and govern your efforts in ways that replenish your energy rather than drain it. Careful energy management will help you to weather the current battle and *and* the next one.

Your dream also affects your cognition. When you begin to embrace your dream on the inside, your thinking will change. You will automatically expand your awareness of what is possible and your thought processes will build in a helpful direction—not on the basis of the opposition you face, but on the dream itself. This produces positive thought momentum at its best. Instead of a tangle of incongruent ideas, one thought will build upon another. This orderly process establishes insight and understanding as to how to conduct your life so that the dream on the inside becomes a reality on the outside.

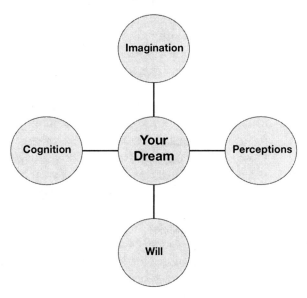

The Will, Excitement, and Resilience

The effects of your dream on your imagination, perception, emotions, and cognition are powerful in building the kind of thought momentum that can lead you out of captivity rather than deeper into it. The effects of your will are also powerful. Your will is yours to assert. How you choose to assert it determines your outcomes.

Your will is not a formula of pre-programmed choices. Instead, it is organic and develops over the course of your lifetime. The foundation stones of your will are your thoughts and beliefs. These serve either to bolster or degrade your will to fulfill your purpose. Thoughts that embrace the realms of possibility support the wise assertion of the will. Negative thoughts generated by a belief in the inevitability of failure, rejection, or loss dilute your will and promote chronic passivity.

The will is vital to your life outcomes for obvious reasons: the exercise of your will yields decisions that shape your life and your direction in life. At every point, you are deciding whether to go this way or that. (Not deciding is a decision, too!) The path you choose will encourage or discourage certain behaviors. These behaviors will in turn shape your future.

You were created for a purpose. That purpose and everything you need to fulfill it have already been planted within you by the Creator. However, *you* have final say as to whether you will finish your course. That final say is exercised through your will. As an act of your will, you are free to choose behaviors that are consistent with your dream. And as an act of your will, you can choose how consistently you will act in beneficial ways!

At any given moment, you have the power to proceed or to give up. You also have the power to maintain a healthy sense of excitement about your dream that will keep you a step ahead of the obstacles that are sure to come. This healthy excitement creates a reservoir of emotional strength that will help you to bounce back from setbacks. That emotional strength is called *resilience*. It is the ability to flex rather than snap under pressure and to rebound from disappointment and discouragement.

If you live in hurricane country, you have probably seen trees whipped by hurricane-force winds. Many trees snap under the pressure; either the winds were too extreme or the tree was vulnerable in some way. A strong, supple tree withstands extreme winds by bending, often dramatically, without breaking. When the storm has passed, the resilient tree is still standing.

Resilience will keep you moving forward for the long haul. It will give you the strength to bounce back when the chips are down and keep moving toward your destiny.

Behave Into Your Destiny

To live your dream, you have to behave your way into your future. If you desire to be a professional football player, you must practice with the same fervor when you are fourteen as you will after you are drafted into the NFL. You must decide to behave in a manner consistent with a destiny that is not yet fully manifested.

Behaving into your future takes faith and tenacity! Joseph suffered grave injustices at the hands of those who should have loved, protected, and supported him. He could easily have become a bitter man with a chip on his shoulder and an axe to grind. We have only touched on a piece of his story; for the record it needs to be said that after being sold and having served as a slave, he was falsely accused of sexual assault (by a married woman whose sexual advances he had refused). As if being a slave was not bad enough, Joseph was thrown into the dungeon.

His circumstances and his dream seemed diametrically opposed. How easy it would have been to succumb to the belief that his dream was over and the walls of his cell would be the last thing Joseph's eyes would see in this life. How many men in his situation would have dreamed of ways to get even? Having been betrayed by his own kin and betrayed yet again by a woman for whom he showed the greatest respect, Joseph could have chosen the path of revenge. But he had a dream. He was destined to be a leader. He was destined, not to harm others, but to benefit them.

Joseph's destiny code was evident in prison: he was assigned a leadership role. Joseph essentially ran the prison! There is only one way he could have been assigned such authority and that is by behaving his way into the future. Instead of groveling, complaining, and lashing out at others, Joseph must have displayed qualities befitting a leader. He had to have shown himself to be of sound mind. He must have demonstrated the ability to make wise decisions. He must have shown himself to be responsible and trustworthy. Instead of being an emotional basket case, Joseph proved himself to be a cut above the rest.

Joseph did all this *before* he was promoted. Instead of acting out on the basis of his past, he behaved his way into his future. This exercise of his will in overriding what must have been a grab-bag of emotions would have monumental implications in the long run. It would position Joseph to become a deliverer to his dream killers—his own family!

Think It Through _____

What life promotion are you seeking? Does your current behavior match your desired destination?

Power to Discover a New Path

When Captain Sullenberger was cleared for takeoff on January 15, 2009, he had a set flight plan and a specific destination in mind. Within moments of leaving the runway at LaGuardia, however, it was clear that the flight plan had changed. Not only was Charlotte out of the question, but Flight 1549 was about to discover an entirely unconventional pathway out of the airspace over New York City.

General MacArthur's words come to mind: "There is no security on this earth, there is only opportunity." In a moment's time, the passengers and crew of Flight 1549 were stripped of any delusions about security in the air. It didn't matter how big, strong, or agile their aircraft was; without engines, it was nothing more than a kite with seats, and an aerodynamically-challenged kite at that. Safety was not assured. Destruction seemed imminent.

In this utter absence of security, Captain Sullenberger, his crew, and his passengers entered a field of opportunity. Would any of them have chosen such a path? Certainly not. Yet, in the midst of what could have been the worst day of their lives—and even the *last* day of their lives—everyone onboard experienced a miracle. The impossible became possible. What looked to be an imminent ending became a new beginning.

Sully became a national hero, an author, and a person of increased influence able to contribute to society in even greater ways. A nation found something to cheer about during its worst financial crisis in more than half a century. First responders who were all too familiar with disaster witnessed an event they could share with their kids and grandkids for years to come. Writers, filmmakers, technicians—people from many walks of life found new opportunities. In the midst of a path that was violently interrupted, new paths were uncovered.

The same happened to Joseph. His life was savagely disrupted. His freedom was stolen. His dreams were trashed by the ones he loved and he was in a place that seemed so far from his expected destination as to boggle the mind.

Yet, Joseph made a choice: he behaved his way into the future and discovered a brand-new path. It did not resemble the one he had envisioned while growing up. It wasn't one he chose to travel. This path demanded of him an adjustment in perspective. It required a resiliency that would enable him to bend and not snap. It forced him to exercise his will to resist the pitfalls of anger, hatred, and bitterness. Joseph's new path pressed him to maintain a healthy sense of excitement about dreams that seemed far out of reach.

Despite their malicious intent, Joseph's brothers were instrumental in bringing his destiny to pass. They fully intended to destroy his life, yet his awful trip to Egypt brought him closer to his destiny. As ugly as the path looked to the naked eye, it was aimed straight at Joseph's destiny fulfillment. The depictions in his dreams were fulfilled in Egypt—a place where Joseph never would have ventured alone by choice.

You cannot discover a new path until you get lost and find yourself headed someplace unfamiliar and even uncomfortable. It is possible that you might never find a real sense of direction until intrusive circumstances thrust you off the path of choice and out of the fog of the comfort zone.

Standing on the edge of the unknown has a way of snapping the slack out of the journey. The very things you would have declined to do under better circumstances can become the experiences that groom you for higher places in life. The things you thought would break you become the precision instruments that help you to focus your vision, energy, and resources on pursuits that are more meaningful and more directly related to the unfolding of your destiny.

The opportunity to discover a new path is a vital element of your destiny code.

Let Go to Move Ahead

Before you can discover a new path to your future, and before you can exploit the opportunities your new path presents, you must first let go of the "old" path and the expectations connected with it.

Captain Sullenberger had to let go of his planned flight path. Had he refused to do so, he would have crashed and burned and taken at least 150 people with him. Because he let go of his expectations of a routine flight ending in Charlotte, he was free to land on the Hudson *safely* after a mind-blowing five minutes in the air.

Letting go demonstrates your willingness to grow and advance through whatever circumstances you encounter. It means releasing something you hold dear, specifically, your version of your future, the outcomes to which you have grown accustomed and to which you have tailored your expectations. It may involve letting go of the job you thought was your ticket to destiny. It may mean dropping a particular expectation regarding the life of one of your children or your spouse. It always means facing a new reality. Often, letting go implies a grief process that must be passed through.

Letting go is part of an emotional continuum. It is a key moment in the end process of having passed through some level of grief, whether over dashed hopes, a material loss, a catastrophic illness or event, or an act of betrayal. Letting go is the signal that you are able to move on. It is the trigger that sets in motion possibilities that await you on the other side of your grief.

At some point in our journey, we all experience grief crises. As unattractive as it sounds, grief is an essential factor in transition. Without the boundaries that grief establishes between a past state and a current one, we will not and cannot let go or move on. In his classic book, *Transitions*, William Bridges describes how transitions serve to move us forward:

> Divorces, deaths, job changes, moves, illnesses, and many lesser events disengage us from the contexts in which we have known ourselves. They break up the old cue system that served to reinforce our roles and to pattern our behavior. It isn't just that the disappearance of the old system forces us to devise a new one, the way that a breakdown in the economic order might lead to barter. It is rather that as long as a system is working, it is very difficult for a member of it to imagine an alternative way of life and an alternative identity. But with disengagement, an inexorable process of change begins....[and] can lead toward a development and renewal.[7]

Transitions extract from us an admission that a particular circumstance (and the security it engenders) is not a permanent condition or final destination. If we embrace them, transitions dissolve our over-reliance on safety nets and comfort zones by forcing us into the unknown places where real living and authentic destiny fulfillment happen.

Letting go and discovering a new path in the cauldron of transition can turn a precocious, pushy kid like Joseph into the world leader he was born to be.

Brace for Your Next Landing

Life is never dull and, if it were, we would cry out for more excitement. Without a dream based in purpose, it is hard to behave your way into the future. Without a destination in mind, your will becomes soft; any choice will do and the easiest route always seems most attractive. Absent a sense of direction, opposing voices become increasingly shrill, thought momentum leads to downward spirals, and resistance to obstacles grows weaker every day. Without any flight plan, your life will end up wherever the prevailing winds take it.

A dream is not enough, however. As we march forward toward destiny fulfillment, we need to be resilient and willing to make adjustments. We need to accept the reality of transition and take from transition the opportunity it offers. Unless our dreams are tempered, we will become rigid when we need to be flexible, reluctant to let go of expectations when destiny unfolds in ways we did not expect. Without realizing it, we will try to inscribe our flight plans in stone and ignore the simple truth that life is very, very fluid.

When you land on your "Hudson" you are faced with a choice: You can rue the change in plans and spend a lifetime immersed in regret and self-pity. Or you can embrace where you are and live it for all it's worth.

Download Your Code

1. How is a sense of security benefiting your life? How might it be hindering you?
2. Describe a rude awakening that turned your life inside out. What effect did it have on your thought momentum and what effect did your thoughts have on the outcome of the crisis?
3. How can the power of your dream to affect your will, perceptions, imagination, and cognition, help you to accurately assess and respond to opposing voices? Give an example from your experience.
4. In terms that are specific to your life, how can you become more resilient? How is your will involved in the process? How will improved resilience affect the unfolding your destiny? Be specific.

5. Can you describe a situation in which your ability or inability to let go affect your discovery of a new path? What drove your approach at the time? How might you approach such a transition differently in the future?

Notes

1. The story of Joseph's life is found in the Book of Genesis, chapters 37 and 39-50.
2. The details of Joseph's story as noted in this chapter are taken from the Book of Genesis, chapters 37 and 39-47.
3. Details are reconstructed from accounts in Dan Mangan, "Hero Pilots Disabled Plane to Safety," New York Post, January 15, 2009, http://www.nypost.com/p/news/regional/item_MjQDz2Utlqls2tD4yZEC0H and William Prochnau and Laura Parker, *Miracle on the Hudson: The Survivors of Flight 1549 Tell Their Extraordinary Stories of Courage, Faith, and Determination* (New York: Ballantine Books, 2009), 37.
4. Mangan.
5. William Prochnau and Laura Parker, *xv*.
6. Chelsey B. Sullenberger III, *Highest Duty* (New York: Harper Collins, 2009), 15-16.
7. William Bridges, *Transitions: Making Sense of Life's Changes, 2nd ed.* (Cambridge, MA: Da Capo Press, 2004), 113.

4
Learning Code-Speak

Learning is not attained by chance.
It must be sought for with ardor and attended to with diligence.

—Abigail Adams

You pull up to the ATM and what do you need? Your debit card and your PIN. Purchase a book online and you better have your user I.D. and password ready, as well as your credit card number and maybe the security code from the back your card. These days, you need a code to do just about anything!

There are codes you are aware of and codes that operate in the background. Computer codes allow you to communicate with your laptop. The computer's native language is the binary system of numbers. If you had to learn your computer's language, your productivity would grind to a halt; so programmers use codes to translate numbers into letters, clicks into actions, key strokes into information.

Think of the lengths you go to where your passwords, PINs, Social Security numbers are involved. You create easy-to-remember codes, record them, memorize them, and lock them in a vault somewhere. You change them periodically, update your list, and memorize them all over again. You keep these codes and all sorts of account numbers handy but safe because they enable you to conduct your business and personal matters with speed and confidentiality—often from remote locations.

Codes are valuable, so we guard them. We know that if we fail to keep our PINs secret, strangers can access our bank accounts and even our medical histories. Businesses, governments, and military institutions rely on codes, passwords, and encryption to keep their information safe, too. Military codes protect national security. Passwords help to secure government installations. Computer encryption keeps business dealings out of the public eye.

Passwords and other secret codes have been used throughout history to gain entrance into the courts of kings, military camps, and even the speakeasies of Prohibition days. Today's codes are high tech by comparison, yet they serve the same purpose: they are gatekeepers. The right code will get you in; the wrong code will lock you out.

Remember, a code is "a system of signals or symbols for communication...."[1] A code is not the information itself. The code is the "language" used to convey the information. This is true of your destiny code. When you understand the language of your destiny code, the signals, symbols, and patterns begin to make sense. When people comment on how articulate you are, you will see it as more than a nice compliment. When organizations invite you to speak, you will recognize the value of your message. When you have a recurring idea about writing a book, you will realize that there is an even larger audience that needs to hear what you have to say.

Little by little, new sections of your path become crystal clear. The farther you walk, the more fluent you become in the language of your destiny code. You become increasingly astute at interpreting new circumstances and events and better prepared for future opportunities.

The converse is also true: If you mistake your destiny code for a never-ending streak of fluke occurrences, you will overlook the meaning that is wrapped inside every life experience. To live the life you truly desire and were created to live, you *must* learn the language of your destiny code.

Destiny Codes Matter

Remember: being lost is a destiny code. If you don't know that, your lost state will look like a disaster from which you must flee. You will react the way most people do: with panic. If you cannot translate the language of the code, the very experience that was designed to unfold the next layer of your destiny will be written off as an embarrassment, a blunder, or worse. Instead of gleaning information from the situation, you will work to forget it ever happened.

Plastic surgeon Francisco Bucio knew enough of the language of the code to persevere when it looked like he should have quit (see Chapter 2). The loss of his hand could have spoken more loudly than what was in his heart—but it didn't. Imagine the long-term impact if it had. It would have been exponential in the negative. His unfulfilled purpose would have affected the life outcomes of people *not yet born!*

What if Joseph had seen his unscheduled journey as a rebuke of his vision? His decision would have potentially aborted the histories of two nations! You see, Joseph's lost season was the lead-up to his being discovered as a wise and gifted leader. Had he not been dragged off to Egypt, he would never have come to the attention of Pharaoh, who literally took Joseph from prison to the palace—where Joseph served as Pharaoh's second in command during one of the region's most difficult periods of famine.[2]

Did you hear that? After years of trial and tribulation, *Joseph became Pharaoh's right-hand man!* The journey was difficult, but it led him to the top. Joseph oversaw Egypt's vast resources and guided her safely through an extended famine. While people outside Egypt starved, Joseph directed the distribution of grain that kept Egyptians alive. On the day of his betrayal, neither Joseph nor his hate-filled brothers realized that he would one day save his own family from starvation *because* he was in Egypt!

Had Joseph misread the destiny code of being lost, he might have perished in the dungeon with nothing but a soul shredded by regret. Egypt and Israel might have perished, too.

Fashion Code

Destiny isn't reserved for world leaders and those called to "select" walks of life. Destiny is encoded in every life for every conceivable purpose. Consider the life of Cynthia Rowley. She created her first dress at the age of seven. Today, she designs everything from women's wear to menswear to airline uniforms, umbrellas, eyeglasses, and home furnishings.[3] The little girl with a dream has become a virtual fashion magnate able to influence culture and industry on a broad scale.

Rowley's destiny continues to unfold in big ways. Her big story began inauspiciously in a Chicago suburb known as Barrington. While most seven-year-old girls long for their parents to buy them pretty dresses; Rowley longed to create dresses of her own. That desire was more than a childhood fancy; it was a destiny code. It signaled Rowley's gifting and purpose. It was a symbol of what was to come. The language of the code revealed that she would one day add color, style, and innovation to the vast marketplace.

In pursuing her passion, Rowley demonstrated fluency in the language of her destiny code. She used her destiny passwords deftly and gained entry to the path that led in the direction of her unique purpose. Step by step, she followed that path through her childhood years and onward.

As a young woman, Rowley attended the Art Institute of Chicago,[4] where her development was presumably encouraged by mentors and fellow students. Commuting to school on Chicago's elevated train system (the El) would have seemed a mundane part of the day for most people. But for Rowley, being an expert navigator of the El was a badge of honor.[5]

Not only that, but she made her daily commute count, especially on a certain day when she wore one of her own designs. That day, a woman on the train noticed Rowley's jacket and started a conversation that would change the young designer's life:

"Cute [jacket], whose is it?"

"Oh, mine! I'm a designer."

"Really? Well here's my card.…Be in my office Monday at 10:10 a.m. with your collection."[6]

The stranger on the train was a fashion buyer for Marshall Field, then a prestigious Chicago department store. Rowley had not yet worked as a designer or created a line of her own. She had, however, dreamed of doing so. Now she had seventy-two hours to make her dream come true. Over the weekend, Rowley created "a capsule collection consisting of three dresses, a tricked-out velveteen jacket, and a two-piece shirt-jacket and cropped-pant matching ensemble."[7]

On Monday morning, the buyer showed an interest in Rowley's collection and asked for garment style numbers:

"What's the style number on that one?"

"Um…one."

"Really? OK. And the style number on *that?*"

"Two."…

"Well, then let me guess…three, four, and five?"

"Exactly!"[8]

Cynthia Rowley knew her lack of experience was showing, but she had read her destiny codes. She knew this was her moment and she capitalized on it. Before the meeting was over, she had her first order—from none other than Marshall Field.[9] In a moment's time, the aspiring designer became a young woman in business, doing exactly what she was born to do.

Destiny and Identity

Remember that destiny is identity. Your destiny code reveals what you were created to do, but always in the context of *who you are*. Rowley must have figured out early on that she wasn't just someone who did…or could…or might design fashion. Design was not just something Rowley *did*. It was a part of who she *was*.

In a metropolis like Chicago, there are, no doubt, many young people who dream of becoming designers. Few achieve the success of Cynthia Rowley. Many never leave the starting gate. There are many reasons for diminished outcomes, but one thing is sure: for destiny to go unfulfilled, a dream has to fall by the wayside. At some point, the pursuit must be abandoned. Perhaps discouragement overshadows the dream. Maybe a lack of belief—in giftedness, in identity, in the value of purpose, or in the codes themselves—makes quitting seem like a wise choice. Somehow, the codes have got to be misread or misused.

You can see why understanding the language of your destiny code is so important. If signals glossed over; if symbols and patterns go unnoticed, substitute paths begin to look attractive and you end up pursuing someone else's dream. Without realizing it, you cobble together a persona that seems to fit your substitute life. You drift from your authentic identity and struggle to fabricate one that is equally seamless. In the end, you will realize that you are trying to do the impossible.

Although you might derive some satisfaction from whatever perks your substitute life provides, there will be a lingering sense that something is wrong. Joy is missing; excitement is lacking. You experience a hunger for something you cannot name. It surfaces regularly until you manage to stuff it so far down as to lose conscious awareness of it. Still the hunger remains; it pops up in other realms. You find yourself seeking satisfaction from people, places, and situations that were not designed to fill your real need. It is a costly, painful, and unrewarding detour.

Nobody wants to end up there. And *you* don't have to!

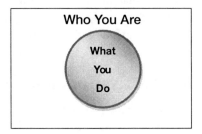

The "Who" of You

At the age of seven, Cynthia Rowley read the language of her destiny code and acted upon it by creating a dress. She did more than enter a field of pursuit; she mounted a lifelong learning curve. Like most destiny achievers, she made an effort to understand the workings of her profession—how do design fashion, how to put garments together, how to run a business.

First and foremost, however, Rowley learned who she was. In the act of pursuing her creative tendencies, she discovered what made her tick. She learned how she was like other kids and how she was different from them. More and more, her pursuit distinguished her from other people and highlighted her unique qualities. Creating that first dress (and every project after that) was an act of *doing* that reflected Rowley's *being*.

When you follow your passions and God-given purposes, you learn about *you*. You discover the organic connection between what you do and who you are. You gain clarity about your direction in life. You know *where* you are going and *why*. Decisions are easier to make. Discouragement is easier to defeat. Criticism yields information and benefit instead of crushing you with feelings of rejection or inadequacy.

The value of understanding yourself cannot be overestimated. It is critical to destiny fulfillment. Until you know who you are, you cannot make a genuine commitment to doing what you were created to do. Unless you understand your identity, you will straddle life's fences, avoid taking risks, and demand your circumstances to line up perfectly before you will make the slightest move.

Knowing yourself improves the quality of your relationships, too. You cannot be understood by others until you understand yourself. That is a loaded statement, so let's explore it: Do you have relationships in which you feel misunderstood? Is it a pattern in your life? Could it be that people are begging for clues as to who you are at your core? Are you providing the guidance they seek or giving them mixed signals because you are not yet sure of your own identity?

Become fluent in the language of your destiny code. Know who you are apart from others, so that you can understand what role you are to play in their lives. Allow the knowledge of your authentic identity to strengthen your commitment to destiny fulfillment. You will be astounded at the places you will go!

Inside-out Living, Motivation, and Self-Respect

When you understand yourself, you can live from the inside out. Here's what that means: instead of being driven by whatever circumstance, influence, or theory comes down the pike, you are powered by an internal generator that acts as both compass and energy source. You don't need things or people to motivate you; your motivation comes from within.

Please understand: I am not advocating a "Lone Ranger" mentality. Having a healthy support system is a good thing. No one can achieve destiny fulfillment without other people playing a part. The issue of inside-out living is about the source of your drive. When you live this way, you tap into the virtual river of motivation that is tied to your purpose. The current keeps you moving in the direction of your destiny future regardless of what other people do or say. Whether or not they support your efforts, your river flows.

You are free to succeed regardless of others, but you must understand this: because your river of motivation affects your outcomes, it will also impact the people around you. They may be your loved ones; they may be the people you don't even who are standing on the other side of your life's purpose. If you are a doctor, they might be your patients and their families. If you are a pastor, they are the people in your church and your community. Whatever your calling, the river flowing inside you will serve to raise the tide for others—for the people you serve, those you mentor, or those who learn from your example. The river inside you always speaks to a destiny that reaches beyond you and your lifespan:

> Although much of life plays out in externals (events, circumstances, wins, losses, etc.), much more of life happens on the inside. Your thoughts, the search for meaning, your inner calling, your destiny codes—they help form a pathway to destiny that leads from the inside out. This path ultimately affects everyone around you and creates a legacy to leave to those who come after you.[10]

When you are motivated by internal forces rather than approval and support of others, you are empowered to succeed under virtually any conditions. Your persistence will often yield the very approval and support you seemed to lack at first. When you move forward from the inside out, it is just a matter of time before you are celebrated by others—often by those you least expect. Even perfect strangers will line up to show their appreciation for who you are and what you do!

The accurate reading of your destiny code produces another powerful effect: When you understand yourself and are empowered to live from the inside out, you learn to respect yourself. No longer do you see yourself through the prism of past hurts, disappointments, and shortcomings, but through the prism of your potential. You learn to regard the purpose you were created to fulfill and, therefore, the vessel that was created to accomplish that fulfillment. *You* are that vessel.

When you respect the person you were created by God to be, you don't have to beg the respect of others. It will be given as a matter of course, in part because you have set an example by respecting yourself.

Think It Through _____

How important is the approval and support of others in your life? Is there any area in which you are waiting for someone or something on the outside to give you the green light to succeed?

Destiny Appointments

Is it difficult to wrap your mind around the idea that an unscheduled meeting on a commuter train can change somebody's life forever? Before she met the buyer from Marshall Field, it might have seemed unbelievable even to Cynthia Rowley.

From all appearances, what proved to be a destiny appointment looked like nothing more than what artist Bob Ross used to call "a happy accident." Neither Rowley nor the buyer had penciled the date on their calendars, yet both of their lives had been moving in a precise direction. Each woman had positioned herself for the unfolding of destiny: the buyer was alert and Rowley silently advertised her talent to the world.

Rowley was not the first design student to cross the buyer's path. But *that* day on *that* train, preparation collided with opportunity. A good fashion buyer always has his or her eyes peeled for something new and promising. The buyer spotted Rowley's jacket, assessed its potential, and took a shot at making something of it. As a result, she landed the budding designer's line—a coup for her store and for her reputation in the industry.

Rowley's enormous success soon testified to the buyer's razor-sharp instincts. But Rowley had done her part, too. She had nurtured her own gift since childhood. She invested time in training so that her gifts could be fully developed. Despite the demands of design school, she took the time to create a garment that would serve as her calling card. This was not an amateurish, hit-or-miss piece of apparel. If it had been, the buyer would not have given it a second glance. No, this was a garment as unique as Cynthia Rowley. It had character. It pointed to talent. And Rowley had the presence of mind to show it off.

Once the buyer offered Rowley an appointment, Rowley made the decision to ride the wave. She didn't make excuses or play herself down. She didn't say, "I'm just a student. I don't have a clothing line. I don't even have experience in the industry. You should probably be talking to someone else."

Rowley never flinched. Offered an appointment on short notice, the young designer accepted it and all that it entailed. And when Marshall Field placed an order, did she back away? No! The logistics must have been overwhelming—she had no factory, no help, and no experience. Yet, she promised to fill the order and found a way to get the job done.

Rowley recognized the value of her destiny appointment. She understood who she was. She was empowered to live from the inside out. She didn't have a manufacturer or a plant of her own or a staff to help her. Still, she was motivated to accomplish the task at hand. She respected herself and her mission; therefore, she knew the effort was worthwhile. Cynthia Rowley hit the ground running and has been a successful designer ever since.

Great story, right? But this book isn't about Cynthia Rowley. *It is about you.* There are destiny appointments in your life. They might not look like Rowley's.

They might not even look like a good thing at first. But if you will honor each and every opportunity as being meaningful, you will find yourself becoming synchronized with your destiny code. Your path might look different from the way you imagined it, but it will take you where you want to go.

Destiny appointments can happen anywhere—in your morning staff meeting, on a first date, or at the supermarket. They can happen while you are walking the dog, helping someone across the street, or getting your hair cut.

Have you ever missed or misread a destiny appointment? Did it look so ordinary that you brushed it off? What can you learn from that experience? What can you do *now* to be ready for the next one? How can you position yourself for the day when preparation and opportunity collide?

Be a Learner for Life

You are beginning to see all that is packed into your destiny code. It is a treasure chest of information ready to fuel your forward progress. Of course, unless you *unlock* the chest, the knowledge it contains will be of no use to you.

Cracking this "safe" is not a one-time event. This is a journey of lifelong learning. Your destiny code doesn't spill out all at once. The information you need to get the ball rolling isn't necessarily the same information you'll need later. As your destiny unfolds, more signals, symbols, and patterns will emerge to urge you forward and help refine your focus.

After she received her "big break" on the elevated train, Cynthia Rowley still had a lot of uncharted territory ahead of her. Even today, with all the success she has under her belt, she has new things to learn and accomplish. If she had closed her destiny codebook on the day of her Marshall Field moment, the only story she would have to tell would be one that happened decades ago.

The way you unlock your destiny code over time is to learn *continually.* It is a process based not on the belief in having arrived, but in the knowledge that you always have someplace farther to go.

The progressive unlocking of your destiny code requires you to be:

Alert to changing information

Diligent to uncover new information

Humble enough to reevaluate your goals

Willing to adapt your methods to changing circumstances

Consistent in maintaining attitudes that are compatible with destiny fulfillment.

Have you ever run into an old friend and been stunned to see her wearing the same hairstyle and makeup she wore twenty years ago? She may have been the most fashionable girl in high school, but her dated look is probably not flattering today. Why? Because the cultural and personal cues that formed the context of her appearance are nowhere to be found now. Big hair was "in." Shoulder pads and big makeup balanced the look. Change the context, and the old look sticks out like a sore thumb.

More importantly, both you and your friend were at different stages in your personal development. Responsibilities and interests evolve as you mature. The youthful priorities and perspectives that inform your choices at eighteen are discarded over time. High school students focus on having fun, drawing attention to themselves, dating, and learning to drive. A lot of learning happens in the decades after graduation.

Your friend's current fashion choices look peculiar because they don't reflect the new things you assume she has learned. Her appearance seems anachronistic, as though her learning process was frozen in time.

Learning is a lifelong interactive process requires you to identify and exploit shifting sources of information. Notice that I said it is an *interactive* process. You can learn only so much while watching TV from your LaZboy. To move toward your destiny, you must expose yourself to new ideas and to people whose viewpoints differ from yours. You must want to learn and you must be willing to let go of the ideas that are no longer working for you.

Your friend with the dated fashion sense must have noticed that the world has changed. Yet she has not allowed the facts to penetrate her fixed ideas. She has chosen to hold on to what she already knows and keep new information (anything that beckons her to change) at arm's length. Based on her decision (whether conscious or not), learning in that area of her life has come to a halt. Instead of adjusting to change, she has forced everything else in her life to adapt to her fixed fashion standards.

Imagine you are taking a history class and are given a textbook containing everything you need to learn. Instead of cracking the book open, you close your eyes, press the book against your forehead, and call it a day. Has your knowledge base changed? Have you interacted with the information you need to pass the class? Of course not! You must open the book, read the pages, take notes, and take another look before exams. You need to process and absorb the information until it becomes part of your repertoire.

Life is a living textbook and learning is an ongoing process. In virtually every moment, you are presented with an opportunity to glean new information from the world around and within you. If you interact with the information, it will add value to your life and nudge you in the direction you need to go. If you need to update your wardrobe, do it. It will affect the way people relate to you. If you need to rethink your management style, do it. It could be the very impetus your staff needs to flourish. If you need to see your children differently, have the courage to make the adjustment.

INFORMATION *d-o-w-n-l-o-a-d-s*

DESTINY *u-n-f-o-l-d-s*

Learn…And Unlearn

We have talked a lot about learning, but there is another process that lasts just as long—it is the *unlearning process.*

Often, we develop expectations based on the facts at our disposal at a given point in time. If you are a widow who dreamed of retiring from the corporate world and opening an antiques shop with your retired husband, you know all too well that facts on the ground can change dramatically and without notice. Grief and loss have rearranged the life you knew and obliterated the future as you envisioned it. The expectations you carried in your heart no longer find a place to "land" in the revised context of your life.

It is a painful and necessary realization. You have come to a crossroad at which you must let go of something. In essence, you must unlearn what you once believed to be a fixed truth about your destiny. The unlearning might pertain to *what* you had in mind. You may have envisioned a certain order of steps: First I get my degree, *then* I begin my career. (This was probably Cynthia Rowley's intent.)

Sometimes the thing you have to unlearn involves the *place* you had in mind. You may have dreamed of being an executive at 3M and ended up being CEO at Dupont. If you are fulfilling your purpose there, accept it. It may be a different place than you had in mind, but it is not the wrong place. Your 3M vision helped you to reach your Dupont destination!

The unlearning process is a critical part of being able to forward. Getting back to the scenario of the unexpected widow, she and her late husband worked together to build a set of expectations regarding their post-retirement lives. It was a worthy endeavor! Their shared picture of the future seemed to fit like a glove. They probably tailored other parts of their lives to dovetail with their developing plan. Neither expected that only one would live to see the plan completed.

When the unexpected happens, you have to do something you never wanted or asked to do: You have to embrace a reality that may be unpleasant at first. You must revise your concept of the future or live in the past. If you are the unexpected widow, you must dig deep to rediscover the river of motivation that continues to flow whether you are attached or alone. If you look beyond your grief and disappointment, you will remember that you have a destiny apart from anybody else's. Your destiny continues to be valid even when loved ones are lost.

Not all transitions involve death and great sorrow. Yet, every transition forces a separation of some kind—from people, beliefs, surroundings, or expectations. In each case, you have to unlearn something that seemed unchangeable. You have to shatter one set of expectations in order to build a new set that allows you to keep growing and living life to the full.

Let's close the chapter with a lighthearted story from William Bridges' book, *Transitions*. It is an example of just how disorienting transitions can be:

> The old radio comedian, Bob Burns ("The Arkansas Traveler"), used to tell the story of eating army food for the first time after eighteen years of his mother's deep-fat frying. A week of bland GI fare was enough to cure something he had never realized he suffered from: heartburn. But rather than feeling relief at his improvement, Burns rushed into the dispensary, clutching his stomach and yelling, "Doc, doc! Help me! I'm dying. My fire went out!"[11]

Burns had not yet learned to read the language of his digestive system. It looked to him like something was terribly wrong. In reality, he had just learned something that would benefit him in the long run. Lifelong learning is not only about what you learn, but about what you need to forget.

It's all in the language of your destiny code.

Download Your Code

1. What experiences or traits do you have in common with Joseph? How does his story help you to learn the language of your destiny coce?
2. Imagine that you are a fledgling designer who must produce a fashion line this weekend and present it to a prominent store on Monday. How do you feel about what you must accomplish? How do you feel about your Monday appointment? Why?
3. Describe one or two ways in which your preparation so far positions you for a destiny appointment. Are there any ways in which a destiny appointment might catch you off guard? Explain.
4. Do you consider yourself to be a lifelong learner? Explain how your life experiences support your answer.
5. Describe a recent situation that forced you to unlearn something. How easy or difficult was it to let go? What was the end result?

Notes

1. Merriam-Webster Online Dictionary 2010, s.v. "code," http://www.merriam-webster.com/dictionary/code (accessed August 17, 2010).

2. Joseph's rise to power and oversight of resources before and during the famine are recorded in the Book of Genesis, chapters 41 and 47.

3. "Fashion's It Girl: An Interview With Cynthia Rowley," Style Chicago, October/November 2007, http://www.stylechicago.com/Category.asp?ID= 11828 (accessed November 6, 2010).

4. Ibid.

5. Cynthia Rowley, Slim: A Fantasy Memoir (New York: Rizzoli International Publications, 2007), 73.

6. Ibid., 74.

7. Ibid.

8. Ibid., 75.

9. Ibid., 76.

10. Mark Chironna, Seven Secrets to Unfolding Destiny (Shippensburg, PA: Destiny Image Publishers, 2010), 74.

11. William Bridges, Transitions: Making Sense of Life's Changes, 2nd ed. (Cambridge, MA: Da Capo Press, 2004), 12.

5
When the Door Slams Shut

When one door of happiness closes, another opens; but often we look so long at the closed door that we do not see the one which has been opened for us

—Helen Keller

Doors open...doors close...doors open. The firstborn child enjoys being the center of attention and—slam!—baby sister comes along and changes everything. The beautiful young actress has her pick of starring roles and then—slam!—"maturity" takes its toll and roles are fewer and farther between.

If you are an adult, you can remember having a killer crush on the girl or boy of your dreams. You believed the sun rose and set on the object of your affections. Then, when you least expected it, the "love of your life" had a change of heart. The door slammed shut on your "happily ever after."

That night, as you cried into your meatloaf and mashed potatoes, a parent shared sage advice: "There are other fish in the sea. You'll find the right person someday."

You didn't care about other fishes or someday. All you saw was door slammed shut on your young dreams. As far as you could tell, it was closed for all eternity.

Light Turns to Darkness

When the door slams shut, an ending is all you see. In the initial darkness, it takes time to reorient and realize that a beginning is taking shape on the other side of your disappointment. It is a pivotal time in which you must feel your way forward: Will you work to recapture the past in which you were invested, emotionally and otherwise? Or will you release your expectations about who, what, when, where, and how, and build new expectations shaped around your unfolding destiny code?

Helen Keller knew a lot about closed doors and dark seasons. When a fever struck and robbed her of both sight and hearing, she entered a titanic struggle to reconnect with the world around her. Submerged in a dark, silent world so early in her young life, she was met with an almost unfathomable ending of the life she had known. Paradoxically, it was also the beginning of an extraordinary story.

Helen Keller's childhood started out like most others:

> The beginning of my life was simple and much like every other little life. I came, I saw, I conquered, as the first baby in the family always does.…
>
> I am told that while I was still in long dresses I showed many signs of an eager, self-asserting disposition. Everything that I saw other people do I insisted upon imitating.…
>
> These happy days did not last long. One brief spring, musical with the song of robin and mockingbird, one summer rich in fruit and roses, one autumn of gold and crimson sped by and left their gifts at the feet of an eager, delighted child. Then, in the dreary month of February, came the illness which closed my eyes and ears and plunged me into the unconsciousness of a newborn baby.[1]

Keller's words send a chill down the spine. Imagine moving from the bright world of childhood to the dark realm of unwilling isolation. Helen continued to grow and interact with others using whatever means she could find, but the older she got, the more frustrating her limited means of communication became.[2]

The quest for expression was complicated by location and technology. Helen's story began in a small Alabama town in 1880. The Kellers had means, but there were few experts and resources available to assist someone with Helen's dual disabilities. Schools for the deaf and blind existed, but none were nearby. Even so, Helen's mother found a glimmer of hope and clung to it. She was "inspired by the story of the successful education of another deaf blind girl"[3]:

> My mother's only ray of hope came from [Charles] Dickens' "American Notes." She had read his account of Laura Bridgman, and remembered vaguely that she was deaf and blind, yet had been educated. But she also remembered with a hopeless pang that Dr. Howe, who had discovered the way to teach the deaf and blind, had been dead many years. His methods had probably died with him; and if they had not, how was a little girl in a far-off town in Alabama to receive the benefit of them?[4]

The challenges Helen's parents faced seemed almost insurmountable. Every door that offered a shred of hope seemed to be shut tightly. Still, the Kellers remained alert. After years without visible signs of progress, their vigilance was rewarded. Helen was six when her father learned of a successful specialist practicing in Baltimore. Without hesitation, Mr. Keller put his family on a train and headed north to meet Dr. Chisholm, a prominent oculist.

The Kellers left Alabama with high hopes. After years of waiting, they would surely have hoped for answers from Dr. Chisholm. Unfortunately, the oculist was unable to help Helen.[5] The first open door they had seen in years slammed shut. Yet, their trip was not wasted. Dr. Chisholm was confident that Helen could be taught if the right teacher or institution were found. He recommended that the Kellers consult with Dr. Alexander Graham Bell in Washington, D.C.[6] (the inventor of the telephone) who was known for his work with deaf children.[7]

The family's travels continued onward to Washington where they met Dr. Bell, who showed Helen great love and kindness. He evaluated Helen and referred the family to Mr. Anagnos, the director of the Perkins Institution in Boston. This was the school connected with Dr. Howe and Laura Bridgman,[8] the names that first kindled Mrs. Keller's hopes! Mr. Keller wrote Mr. Anagnos at once and requested assistance in finding a teacher for Helen. Once again, the Kellers waited patiently.

> …in a few weeks there came a kind letter from Mr. Anagnos with the comforting assurance that a teacher had been found. This was in the summer of 1886. But Miss Sullivan did not arrive until the following March."[9]

The Power of Resolve

Since the onset of Helen's illness and resulting disabilities, the Kellers had traveled a rough road. Few prospects presented themselves. With each passing day, the door to Helen's future seemed more rigidly jammed in the closed position. Now, a crack had opened. A welcome shaft of light shined through the crack and illuminated a new beginning for Helen.

Now, it was a matter of waiting for the arrival of Ann Sullivan, the woman whose destiny it was to draw Helen Keller out of the dark silence and into a full and rewarding future. Of course, that would prove to be a journey with a story all its own.

Do you remember our discussion of opposing voices in Chapter 3? Even when our most brilliant opportunities appear, voices of doubt and fear clamor for our attention. For a family whose little girl had been stripped of her senses, those voices were backed up by history: bad outcomes were familiar territory to the Kellers. Voices of fear and doubt might easily have convinced them that a good outcome was not possible. Yet, they persevered. They had followed through on every lead prior to the hiring of Ann Sullivan. After her arrival, they endured new challenges, always hopeful of the day when Helen's loss would be redeemed.

In his article, "The Power of Resolve," Dr. Alex Lickerman writes:

> If we pause for a minute to consider all the obstacles Arthur and Kate Keller had to overcome to find and follow this convoluted path to Annie Sullivan—in the late 1800s no less—we're led to conclude that they must have had an abundance of the very same stuff that enabled Helen herself not only to learn to communicate but also to become the first blind person to earn a Bachelor of Arts degree ever (at Radcliffe), to read Braille (not only in English but also French, German, Greek, and Latin), to write and publish numerous books, to campaign for women's suffrage, for worker's rights, and for socialism, and even to help found the ACLU— namely, resolve.[10]

Against the odds, Helen Keller learned to do what came easily to most other young girls her age—and then exceeded their accomplishments. Helen Keller found a way to excel in ways that most sighted, hearing people never do!

This is the power of resolve. Whether or not you agree with every cause Helen Keller championed, it is clear that she and her family were driven from within to overcome extraordinary challenges. Through persistence, they silenced the voices, even those in their own family that said Helen might be beyond reach.[11] When Helen's frustration manifested in tantrums and other outbursts, they managed the mounting tension. When it seemed there would always be another step between them and the help Helen needed, they summoned the strength to take that step.

The power of resolve will keep you focused on your desired outcome instead of on the challenges piled up along your path. Resolve is the difference between wishing for something good to happen and being determined to accomplish it.

---

re·solve

noun

1. a resolution or determination made, as to follow some course of action.
2. firmness of purpose or intent; determination.[12]

The Recipe for Resolve

Dr. Lickerman describes three necessary ingredients of resolve that will help you to assess your strengths or weaknesses in this area. This is not an exhaustive study, but a good primer on the subject of resolve.[13]

1. Passion for your goal—Without a passion to see their daughter's life restored, the Kellers would have been less likely to extend themselves without some advance evidence that their efforts (expense, travel, and contacts) would prove worthwhile.

Resolve is related to faith. You might not realize that you need it until you are faced with something you perceive to be "bigger" than you or beyond your ability. You can get by without resolve you are willing to live a lifestyle of getting by. You don't need resolve to throw a load of clothes into the washer and press "Start." You hit the button and walk away, confident that your clothes will be laundered while you are doing other things.

The need for resolve becomes evident when you have five children, the hamper is piled to the ceiling with dirty clothes, you work sixty hours a week, your washer is on its last legs, and you don't have the money to replace it. Suddenly, you have to find a way where there seems to be no way. Without resolve, you cannot get "there" from "here."

2. The ability to ignore the odds—Dr. Lickerman talks about the hidden benefits of incompetence, explaining that those who are unaware of their shortcomings also tend to be unaware of the odds stacked against them. This blissful ignorance keeps them from getting wrapped around the axle of self-doubt and gives them a hidden advantage against their more skilled competitors, provided they develop essential skills along the way.[14]

For those who are painfully aware of the obstacles, success is a matter of managing the negative chatter that crosses your radar screen. Consider the way Captain Sullenberger took command of his thought momentum in the dwindling moments of Flight 1549. Lights were flashing; warnings bellowed; altimeters confirmed the obvious. Questions raced through the minds of Captain Sullenberger and his crew. Passengers prepared themselves for impact.

Sullenberger heard the voices of doom, but resisted their demand for attention. He knew the odds were stacked against him, but he chose to invest his faith and all of his energy into the possibility, however small, of a good outcome. With an impenetrable sense of resolve, he fixed his mind on finding solutions and converted a catastrophe into a celebration. Imagine how the story of Flight 1549 would have ended if the captain had not bucked the odds!

3. Endurance—Resolve implies the decision to endure. If you have resolved to achieve a given end, you have determined that you will finish what you started. This kind of determination typically meets with some form of resistance. Obstacles will surely arise; setbacks will knock the wind out of your sails. The test of your resolve will be shown in the level of your endurance. Will you get back up after a nasty fall, or will you retreat to the path of least resistance?

Consider the Wright brothers. Their interest in flight began when "their father brought them a toy 'helicopter.'…Made of cork, bamboo, and paper, with a rubber band to twirl its twin blades, it was a little bigger than an adult's hand. They later said this sparked their interest in flight. During the next few years, Wilbur and Orville tried to build these themselves, but the bigger they made them the less well they flew. Somewhat discouraged, the brothers turned to kites."[15]

In later years, the brothers began experimenting with gliders:

In 1901, at Kill Devil Hills, North Carolina, the Wright Brothers flew the largest glider ever flown, with a 22-foot wingspan, a weight of nearly 100 pounds and skids for landing. However, many problems occurred: the wings did not have enough lifting power; forward elevator was not effective in controlling the pitch; and the wing-warping mechanism occasionally caused the airplane to spin out of control. In their disappointment, they predicted that man will probably not fly in their lifetime.[16]

There was a moment in time when the Wright brothers thought the door to their dream had closed. It is not surprising that they experienced a period of doubt. Every champion does. Yet, their destiny codes continued to crank out the fundamental belief that man could fly. This helped them to endure. They recognized failed experiments as part of the process that leads to success. They had been knocked down several times, but refused to stay down.

The Wright brothers had a sense of resolve that ensured the completion of their goal—to fly!

I agree with Dr. Lickerman that "we all have the power to summon up an inflexible will to win."[17] Resolve is not the sole property of those we ordain has having been born to win. Resolve is a decision each of us can make. It allows for strength and makes room for our potential to blossom. Resolve is a means to an end, but it is choice made before we have tangible proof that success is coming.

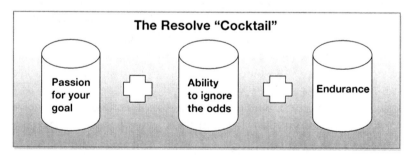

The Beautiful Burden

Invite people to a seminar about burden-bearing and few will show up. The word *burden* feels heavy, like something to be avoided. Some burdens *are* to be avoided. The burden of debt comes to mind. The phrase summons to mind strong images of people dragging loads of bricks behind them, weary and exhausted from pulling the load.

A burden demands decisions. If my cell phone rings when I am encumbered with sacks of groceries, I will probably let voicemail handle the call. When I carry an infant, I focus on holding him tightly and watching my step as I make my way down the stairs. If I am laden with debt, I must choose to avoid discretionary purchases so I can pay down my balance.

When you carry a load of any kind, your priorities change. If you operate as though the burden were not there, you end up with a bigger load to carry.

---

bur·den

noun

1: something that is carried…load…duty, responsibility

2: something oppressive or worrisome

3: the bearing of a load…[18]

Let's establish an important point about burdens: the right burdens are necessary ingredients to a rich, rewarding life. Often, it is easy to distinguish between "bad" burdens and "good" ones. The burden of debt is an obvious downer. Each month demands that you jump through a series of financial hoops and kiss your hard-earned money goodbye. But the burden of carrying an infant is a delight. The fresh scent of his hair, the cooing sounds he makes, and the way his tiny hands explore your face—you wish you could carry him forever!

Some of life's beautiful burdens are carried by people everywhere: the commitment of marriage; the raising of children; the responsibilities associated with job, business, or ministry; the maintenance of the home; the care of physical and spiritual health. Everything in this list is something to which you consent because you desire to do so. You fall in love, marry, and start a family. You are fortunate to be able to work; you choose a career or a position and you bear your responsibility to fulfill the duties that come with it. You are blessed to have a roof over your head that requires attention and upkeep. You get the idea.

There are specific, often unique burdens associated with your destiny code. No one can carry your burdens but you. If your dream is to be a gold-medal winning figure skater, you will spend countless hours on the ice. You will begin training in childhood and continue to train throughout your career, both as an athlete and a dancer. To remain competitive, you will need to raise the bar on your technical performance, learning the latest jumps, spins, and lifts. You know that a plateau mind-set will ensure an early retirement. You will take good care of your body: you will eat smart, condition yourself for endurance and strength, and take the steps needed to prevent injury.

Other requirements are needed for you to make the cut. You need to be mentally tough, able to withstand public scrutiny and the emotional roller-coaster of competing at a high level. Travel is a must; therefore you must adjust to living out of your suitcase. And if you want to grow up the way other kids do, you will soon learn that your childhood and dating years will be anything but "normal."

That is quite a load! But if you have a passion for skating, you consider it a privilege to carry your burden with you through life. Nothing about it is easy; but the rewards cannot be described with words. In the difficult moments, when the urge to complain rises in your throat, you pull out the mental "big picture" that carried you this far. You view the current challenge in the context of your dream, and you decline the opportunity to mutter and moan.

Why? Because bucking the burden disqualifies you from bearing it and all of the blessing it promises to yield. Griping will chip away at your resolve and dilute your will to succeed. If you see the burden as being unfair or unworthy, your subconscious mind will seek alternate routes to the destiny you claim to desire. You will eventually entertain those routes and the ease they promise. In the end, your substitute destiny will leave you wanting.

Your self-disqualification also speaks to those around you. It is a potent, but silent press release that says, "I cannot be trusted with this opportunity. My reluctance to bear this burden will eventually sabotage the dream I profess to hold dear."

The people you need to help fulfill your destiny will no longer be attracted to your cause. Your mentors will continue, at least for a time, to encourage and affirm the burden. But, unless you demonstrate an enduring willingness to rise to the level of greatness and fulfill your calling to yourself and to those you are assigned to influence, the best mentor will eventually stand down. Why? Because mentors desire to fulfill their destinies, too. Once your surrender is clear, they will find willing destiny achievers to encourage and affirm.

Think It Through _____

Describe your destiny burden. What does your choice of adjectives tell you about what this burden means to you?

Choose Your Battle

Let's face it: life involves warfare. Whether you are rich or poor, famous or unknown, you will fight your share of battles. No matter where you see yourself on the world's "totem pole," the war for your destiny is engaged—and you have just one lifetime in which to win it.

Although everyone is involved in this war, some battles are better than others. I often hear people say, "I've been poor and now I'm rich. Rich is better." *Better* does not mean "without a care in the world." It means the war you wage will produce something more than mere survival. The war for success and prosperity creates more choices for you and your loved ones and those you are called to serve.

Millions of honorable people struggle day in and day out under the weight of poverty. Every moment produces another need that seems out of reach: the rent is due; diapers are running low; the electric company is threatening a shut-off; you are out of milk for the kids; your car is running on empty. Months roll in and months roll out without so much as a hint of forward motion. The only thing you can count on is the status quo of *not enough*. It is a never-ending battle to live within life's closed doors.

The continual, recurring challenges of survival are exhausting. You expend enormous amounts of energy—not honing your gifts or blessing others with your talents; not deciding which house to buy or which charity to endow—but wondering where your next meal is coming from and how you will avoid becoming homeless. You will work hard and try your best to make it to the next day, yet your true potential will go unexploited.

In this life, you can rest assured that you will wage war either way: You will fight unending battles for survival or you will fight for the fullness of your destiny. I am convinced the latter is the better choice because it is a battle to *expand* your horizons by blasting *through* life's closed doors. As different as these wars are, both are fought on the fields of everyday life. Sometimes, it will be difficult to distinguish one battle from the other. Still, you must choose. No one can force your hand.

If you choose to fight for your destiny, you must first stake out your claim. You acknowledge your destiny code and you engrave it upon your heart. You pledge (to yourself and to those who will hold you accountable) your resolve to fight to the finish. You put on your armored vest and your camos and you patrol the field of your destiny—day in and day out.

Once you enter the battlefield, you have to allow the facts on the ground to affect your battle plan. You will need to break out from the strategies and tactics that no longer work. Military strategists will tell you that even the best laid battle plans become casualties to war's opening salvo. War requires flexibility. You must hold on to your vision, but continually adjust your battle plan to shifting circumstances. That is a winning plan.

French statesman Georges Clemenceau said, "War is a series of catastrophes that results in a victory."[19] When one catastrophe seems to follow on the heels of another, keep your eyes focused on victory. Remain determined to see the battle through to its glorious conclusion. Move beyond the fight for survival and fight the good fight for your destiny.

1. Choose Your Battle:
   Destiny or Survival?

2. Stake Your Claim
   (Read Destiny Code)

3. Resolve to Win

4. Adjust Battle Plan

Train for the Invisible Realm

Much of life plays out in the physical world. You drive a car, eat food, and sit in a chair. Even if you don't understand the intricacies of combustion, chemistry, and physics, you know your car will get you to work, your body needs nourishment, and the dining room chair was designed to hold your body weight.

We are well-trained to function in the physical realm. We are quick to say, "Seeing is believing." What we are saying is, "When I see an outcome, I will accept it as fact. Until then, I reserve judgment."

There is practical wisdom in this approach. You don't spend money you have yet to earn. You don't punish your children before they commit offenses that warrant reprimand. You don't run the lawnmower before the grass comes up. We rely on sound physical evidence to make good decisions in our everyday affairs.

However when it comes to war, you need to have more working for you what you can see, hear, touch, feel, taste, and smell. Left unchecked, the need for physical evidence can be detrimental. This idea is captured so well by a quote from the Latin epic poem *The Aeneid* by Virgil: "They can conquer who believe they can."[20]

In the end, our outcomes are decided as much by what we believe as by what we do. Beliefs, attitudes, inspiration—these exist in the realm of the invisible. It is the place where much of destiny unfolds (and a topic unto itself). For now, it is important to realize that the invisible realm exists and profoundly affects your life.

Although you cannot touch the yearnings that stir deep in your heart, you know they are there. You cannot take a photograph of your skepticism, but it leaves its imprint on your outcomes. No matter how well-trained you are to function in the physical realm, your physical life alone cannot produce destiny fulfillment. The Wright brothers knew a lot about the physics of flight. If that was all that was needed, the company that produced the toy helicopter might have beaten the Wright brothers into the history books. Instead, the Wright brothers turned the toy into inspiration and followed through to achieve something greater.

The Wright brothers reached into the realm of the invisible.

We were born to function in the invisible realm, but most of us have little practice functioning in that domain. Therefore, we are more comfortable operating on the basis of what our physical senses tell us. We ask our senses to dismiss our doubts and give us permission to move forward with our plans, even though the battle for destiny is ultimately won or lost in the area of belief.

Helen Keller could not have overcome the overwhelming obstacles she faced *and* lived an extraordinary life of accomplishment without tapping into the invisible realm. Likewise, the most gifted skater would not stand a chance of winning Olympic gold absent the mind-set that allows an individual to rise above the competition.

Root Out Self-Sabotage

If the script that is running in your head (and we all have scripts running in our heads) says, "Every time I get to the big competitions, I miss the triple axel and crash to the ice," your skill won't save you from defeat. The thoughts operating in the background of your mind will sabotage your desire to win. You will walk away from center ice scratching your head and wondering how you could make such a costly mistake.

Another variety of self-sabotage is the never-ending waiting game. King Solomon described it perfectly in just eighteen words: "He who watches the wind will not sow and he who looks at the clouds will not reap."[21]

A wise farmer is always aware of the weather. He knows that he will maximize his crop if he sows and reaps at the right time and regulates irrigation in response to weather patterns. Solomon was not averse to the wise monitoring of the skies. The problem he addressed was one of degree. Yes, farmers must follow the weather, but if a farmer wants a guarantee that the weather will cooperate perfectly, he will never plant his seed. If he so fears the loss of his harvest that he waits for every last cloud to leave Planet Earth, his crop will go to seed and be lost for sure.

We have to recognize the realm of the invisible—the realm of thoughts and beliefs and the willingness to take risks—and train our brains to harness that realm for our benefit. You cannot wait for the right results to convince you of your destiny code. You trust what your destiny code reveals and act on it.

Your destiny codes are felt in your heart, where feelings of pain and joy testify to their existence. If you are called as a missionary to the people of Costa Rica, your heart will stir with excitement when you hear the place mentioned or have an opportunity to donate to the needs of the people there. Your heart will break when you read about the trials of Costa Ricans. You will become impatient when your plans to relocate to the mission field are delayed. Your heart will stir with emotions that separate you from everyone else. They will see the same photos as you; they might even donate to the same cause; yet they will forget about Costa Rica and move on to something else while you are still carrying a burden for the people in your heart.

Your heart dreams your future into existence, to the extent that you believe it. The visible world as you know it exists because of an invisible reality. Regardless of your view of the Creation, you know that the skyscraper in which your office is located began as a vision in someone's mind. When you grasp this reality, you position yourself to experience the complete unfolding of your destiny code.

When a stranger on a train asks you about the self-designed jacket you are wearing, your destiny antennae will reach into the invisible realm and summon everything you need to follow through with the opportunity. Self-confidence will arise, resources will be found, creativity will be ignited, and your gifts will flourish. Your dream will be manifested because you believed it was possible.

Your mind has to be taught what your heart already knows. Then you have to apply that knowledge to your life. Your heart knows more about you than you consciously realize. When your mind and your heart are guided by the same information, there is nothing you cannot accomplish. You train your brain by first becoming aware of the destiny code in your heart and then downloading it to your mind. Your dream is more than encouraging; it is destiny-producing because it alters your sense of what is possible. This knowledge in turn alters your behavior. You believe your dream is possible and you began to act in ways that are born of your belief. You apply what you believe to the physical realm of your life through an act of your will, which is now bolstered by belief in your destiny.

Your behavior is the fruit of your beliefs. If you believe you are going to a place called Nowhere, you will see signs for Nowhere every place you go. Absent the knowledge of your destiny code, you see only your inadequacies and the odds that are stacked against a glorious outcome.

But when your destiny code is fixed in both your mind and your heart, you will shape and develop your behavior around what you believe about your future. You will organize your life, not around the ever-shifting circumstances of the everyday, but around the information your destiny code has revealed. You will reach into the invisible realm just as Helen Keller and the Wright brothers did.

When your expectations of your destiny are based on the God-given destiny code in your heart...and when your mind is trained to follow what is in your heart, behaving your way into the future is as easy as breathing in and out.

Victory will be just a matter of time.

Download Your Code

1. Which is the most recent door that seemed to slam shut in your life? How did you feel when it happened? How did you respond? How might you respond differently in the future?

2. Do you agree with the statement, "Resolve is a decision each of us can make"? Explain. How is your belief in this statement reflected in your outcomes?

3. What was your most visceral reaction (whether positive or negative) to our discussion of burdens? What beliefs about burdens did you bring to this chapter? How were they changed?

4. Describe what you see when you envision yourself as a warrior in the battle for your destiny. What surprised you in this mental picture? Explain.

5. You have heard it said that a house divided is doomed to fall. How can you relate this truth to our discussion of the mind, heart, and behavior? Did you discover any internal divisions operating in your life?

Notes

1. Helen Keller, *The Story of My Life* (New York: Bantam Dell, 2005), 3-4.
2. Ibid., 11.
3. Alex Lickerman, M.D., "The Power of Resolve," *Psychology Today* online, November 26, 2009, http://www.psychologytoday.com/blog/happiness-in-world/200911/the-power-resolve (accessed November 6, 2010).
4. Keller, 11.
5. Ibid., 11-12.
6. Ibid., 12.
7. Lickerman.
8. Keller, 13.
9. Ibid.
10. Lickerman.
11. Keller, 11.
12. Dictionary.com Unabridged Random House, Inc., s.v. "resolve," http://dictionary.reference.com/browse/resolve (accessed: September 24, 2010).
13. The following three steps are based on Dr. Lickerman's article, "The Power of Resolve," cited above.

14. Lickerman.

15. "The Wright Brothers: Wilbur and Orville Wright," wright-house.com, http://www.wright-house.com/wright-brothers/Wrights.html (accessed September 24, 2010).

16. Mary Bellis, "History of Flight: The Wright Brothers," About.com: Inventors, http://inventors.about.com/od/wstartinventors/a/TheWrightBrother.htm (accessed September 24, 2010).

17. Lickerman.

18. Merriam-Webster Online Dictionary 2010, s.v. "burden," http://www.merriam-webster.com/dictionary/burden 9/25/10 (accessed September, 25, 2010).

19. The Quotations Page, "Georges Clemenceau 1841-1929," http://www.quotationspage.com/quotes/Georges_Clemenceau/(accessed November 6, 2010).

20. Virgil, Aeneid, http://www.quotationspage.com/subjects/belief/ and P. Virgilius Maro: Aeneidis libri I - VI, Volume 2 - Page 644 (Bibliotecha Regia Monacensis, 1803, http://books.google.com/books?id=5wg-AAAAcAAJ&pg=PA644&dq=poffunt+quia+poffe+videntur&cd=1#v=onepage&q=poffunt%20quia%20poffe%20videntur&f=false for original quote in Latin.

21. Ecclesiastes 11:4 (New American Standard Bible).

6

Bottom's Up

And so, suddenly, there they were, vigorous and exultant and newly thankful for the privilege of walking atop God's orb.

—New York Daily News Editorial, October 14, 2010

At the time of this writing, the world celebrates. Thirty-three Chilean miners are enjoying freedom and fresh air on the surface of the earth after being trapped in her bowels for sixty-nine harrowing days.

This outstanding story of adversity and redemption will continue to unfold in the months and years to come. Book and movie deals are already in the offing; but the freed miners have made a pact: they will keep the rest of their story under wraps until all opportunities can be sorted out. Having survived the ordeal as a group, they are determined to share equally in the windfall that seems to await them.

What a contrast to the bleak beginnings of their saga when a rock fall occurred, trapping the men. For the next seventeen days, no one knew the fate or exact location of the miners. Each day, the odds of rescuing the men alive diminished. Yet, the miners' loved ones never gave up hope. They literally camped out at the site, erecting a makeshift tent village aptly named *Camp Hope*. In no time at all, the temporary residents developed "zones for children, community bulletin boards, scheduled bus shuttle services to nearby cities...."[1]

Meanwhile, experts from around the world offered to help. Drilling specialists dug exploratory holes through thousands of feet of dense rock. Crews worked tirelessly to find signs of life. They were well aware of the obstacles and unwilling to give up on the souls trapped below. For more than two weeks, the miners' fate remained unknown. But on the seventeenth day, rescuers made a joyous discovery:

> ...rescuers were shocked when they pulled a drill bit out of a hole drilled into a refuge chamber only to find notes stuck on the end of it with insulation tape.[2]

It was a miracle! All thirty-three men were alive and in good condition! Now, the goal was to keep them alive and return them to the surface. But how? And how long would it take? The miners had survived, but they remained at risk. Time was of the essence, but everyone knew there was no quick fix.

Those above ground and below coalesced around the cause. Destiny codes fired on all cylinders as scientists, engineers, psychologists, doctors, nutritionists—everyone including the miners—applied themselves and their skills to the monumental task at hand. An international effort was underway.

In the mine, the men rallied around a leader, a man gifted to keep them on track. Assignments were handed out; tasks were scheduled; lines of communication were organized. Medical issues were addressed and critical supplies were ferried through a five-inch wide tunnel. A diary was kept and a poet wrote about the men's experiences. Bibles were requested and prayer meetings were organized. Under difficult circumstances and the watchful eye of a video feed, the men carried on below while those above ground watched, worked, and waited.

Atop the mine and around the world, men and women sought the best methods available to do what seemed to be impossible. Time projections were made and the miners were told they would likely remain in the hole for four months![3] The implications of extended confinement were worrying. Even NASA got involved by providing expertise about the physical, emotional, and psychological effects of isolation and confinement to close quarters. At best, the men's health could be compromised. At worst, another collapse could entomb them forever.

Day in and day out, drillers worked to widen the exploratory tunnel. The miners' location was hard to reach; bends and curves in the tunnel would extend the drilling time and make egress difficult. Engineers devised a rescue capsule to shuttle the miners to the surface, one man at a time. The vehicle was just wide enough to quite literally encapsulate one person. It would be a slow, dark, solitary journey to the top. Claustrophobia and technical glitches seemed almost inevitable.

Imagine the many destiny paths that converged at the San Jose mine! Consider the life experiences, the educational histories, the entrepreneurial ventures, the myriad levels of preparedness that preceded this call to arms. Every man and woman involved had been walking toward this moment *for years*, each one bringing to the table the gifts, knowledge, and confidence that had been developed over the course of a lifetime!

The survival of the miners would not be achieved by luck. Both the men and their rescuers contributed to the hoped-for good outcome in a very conscious manner. Despite the trauma they had suffered, the trapped men assumed a pro-active stance. This can be seen in the fastidious rationing of their resources during the first seventeen days of their confinement:

> Each of the 33 miners trapped a half-mile underground lived on two spoonfuls of tuna, a sip of milk, a bite of crackers and a morsel of peaches. Every other day.

> They were so careful in eating what was supposed to be a two-day emergency supply that when the outside world finally reached them 17 days after a mine collapse, they still had some food left.[4]

For the miners, survival required a conscious effort, smart decision-making, the setting of sound goals, and the will to make it for as long as it would take to get from the bottom of the world back to the top.

The effort would prove well worth it.

The Meaning of *Meaning*

While they were separated from the rest of world, the Chilean miners would surely have asked new questions about the meaning of life. Having cheated death in the original rock fall, their perspectives of life would necessarily have shifted. In their stark circumstances—and even for their loved ones above ground—the inherent value of life would have been in the front of every mind. Survival and another chance were all that mattered. It was a common goal. As a group, the men cooperated with one another and with that goal. They did whatever they could do to emerge from the dark hole of their captivity.

Crises have a way of making matters transparent. With survival as your goal, the minutiae of life are forced to the back burner. The small stuff you might sweat while on the surface can't touch you here. How ironic it is to discover that living under intense constraints can bring new freedom. With the clutter removed, it is easier to make the big-picture choices that line up with your destiny code.

Even crises have positive fallout. Yet, crises aren't the only way to find clarity. Our lives have meaning and purpose even when we are distracted by the cares of the world. When we feel trapped in a hamster-wheel existence, we can dig deep into our God-given destiny codes and find the motivation and information needed to rise in the direction of destiny fulfillment.

Do you remember the bestseller by Rick Warren entitled *The Purpose Driven Life*? The book sold tens of millions of copies around the world. It was a terrific book, but why did it become the second-biggest seller of all time, apart from the Bible? I believe it is because we are living in a time when meaning and significance are elusive. Millions bought the book out of a sense of unspoken desperation. They wanted to know the answer to life's most fundamental question: *Why am I here?*

It is a paradox that, in this age of information, the search for meaning is more daunting than ever. The search is not new; we were created to find meaning, even when nothing seems to make sense.

> We are natural born meaning-makers. Have you ever noticed your irritation when someone says or does something that, in your mind, makes no sense? How do you respond? Do you force the issue by demanding an explanation or do you mull over it again and again searching for a window into the offender's train of thought?

> …This search for meaning is connected to our identity as spiritual beings. Regardless of the position you take on faith, religion, and deity, you naturally seek for meaning that extends beyond yourself. We all desire to understand our connection to something bigger and less fleeting than our brief lives and physical limitations.[5]

This is the quest of every human being. Consider Holocaust survivor Viktor Frankl who grappled with life's meaning during an upheaval of the highest magnitude. Having experienced great loss, deprivation, and disorientation during the Holocaust, Frankl was determined to understand what happened and to discover his purpose in light of his extreme experiences. Frankl reached the following conclusion:

> Man's search for meaning is the primary motivation in his life and not a "secondary rationalization" of instinctual drives. This meaning is unique and specific in that it must and can be fulfilled by him alone; only then does it achieve a significance, which will satisfy his own will to meaning.[6]

"Meaning determines purpose."[7] Frankl found meaning and purpose in the midst of his trauma:

> Making use of his time as a prisoner in several concentration camps, Frankl worked to bring hope to those who were distraught. After the liberation, he learned that [his wife] Tilly had perished. He was devastated and considered suicide. Yet, because he was convinced of a greater purpose for his life, he rejected the thought of killing himself saying, "When all this happens to someone, to be tested in such a way,…it must have some meaning. I have a feeling…that I am destined for something."[8]

Frankl interpreted his destiny code in the midst of the most unreasonable circumstances. Yet even the insanity of the Holocaust did not cause him to deny his destiny; instead it provided evidence that he had a destiny—and a significant one at that:

> Frankl was right. As a free man, he wrote and lectured about the psychology of the concentration camps and about the characteristics of those who managed to survive. He found meaning in the awful experience of the Holocaust by using it as a metaphor with which to bring others into wholeness.[9]

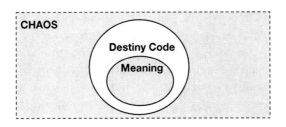

There are vast differences between the experience of the Holocaust and the collapse of a copper mine. Yet, there are parallels as regards the search for meaning. How the Chilean miners handle the balance of their lives cannot be seen as of this writing. We do know this much: regardless of their viewpoints, shortcomings, and emotional tendencies prior to the mine collapse, they saw life through a new lens and they saw it for what it is—*a gift.*

Conscious Cooperation

Let me make this point before we continue: a life-changing experience is not the solution to every problem. Some old problems greeted the Chilean miners almost as soon as the fresh air hit their faces. But traumatic experiences bring things into focus—and fast. Do you need to be trapped underground to gain that kind of focus? No. All you need is to unearth your destiny code and consciously cooperate with it.

Life is fluid and every experience creates ripples. These ripples are often inconvenient. Unexpected things happen. Results—even good outcomes—are often something other than what you had in mind. You can choose to get in the flow or resist the changing currents. You can choose to cooperate with your unfolding destiny or you can try to frame a life that looks the way you think it should look.

You can force the issue, but it will cost you. To achieve destiny fulfillment, you must cooperate with your destiny code. Even before they had any tangible hope of being rescued, the Chilean miners cooperated with their desired end result. They did the little things that kept them on top of their game until freedom came knocking. It was a fishbowl experience in which every movement mattered.

The men's choices served them well underground. But even their rescue was not the end of the story. Once freed, they were plunged into the international limelight. Now, they have new issues to work through. It will be important for them to grasp their destiny codes and cooperate with them—even when the demands of celebrity and sudden wealth threaten to draw them off course.

You cannot turn back the hands of time. Life's changes cannot be undone. This is true whether you were trapped underground for sixty-nine days or lost your job of twenty-five years. Every change generates new information. Every shift leads in the direction of unfamiliar circumstances that must be navigated. All of it is part of your destiny code. You can resist the process when it becomes uncomfortable, or you can cooperate with it and reach a better destination than even you had in mind.

The key to steadfastly cooperating with your destiny code is to view all circumstances from the perspective of your destiny fulfillment. If you fail to grasp this big picture view, you will find yourself at odds with your desired outcomes. You will have no reference point from which to tackle the "impossible"; you will lack the motivation to plow through the unpleasant parts of your assignment; you will unwittingly forfeit future rewards. You might never know in this lifetime just how much you gave up—all because you opposed the very destiny code you claim to value.

The Chilean miners longed to be reunited with their families, but they could have inadvertently opposed such an outcome. Imagine if they had allowed the frustrations of their situation to fester. What if they had engaged in turf wars underground or fought over food supplies or leadership roles? Any form of division could have compromised the survival of one or more of the men.

Cooperation with destiny, even under difficult conditions, is a prerequisite to its fulfillment.

Choices Revisited

How does destiny cooperation play out in the real world? It happens in your choices. Your decision-making will reveal whether you are cooperating with or resisting your destiny code.

We have talked about choices in a variety of contexts: We know that new choices become evident during crises. We have discussed the importance of choosing our thoughts and managing thought momentum. We watched how destiny-fulfillers Francisco Bucio, Chelsey Sullenberger, and others responded when their available choices became few and unattractive. We learned about choosing which battle to fight: the battle to survive or the battle for destiny fulfillment. Most importantly, we learned that choices are always available and are always ours to make.

The key is to make the conscious choices that cooperate with our destiny codes. For the Chilean miners, cooperation meant accepting a period of deprivation, particularly in the first seventeen days of their isolation beneath the earth. If they had not strictly and fairly rationed their small stash of tuna and milk, they might not have lived to see their rescue. They were *committed* to cooperating.

Absent this commitment, you can "talk the talk" of your dreams for a lifetime and still not see them fulfilled. Yes. You *can* long for your destiny and still not experience it. You must become conscious and deliberate—aware of your surroundings; determined to be proactive; and willing to make the tough choices that promote destiny completion. To live your dream, you must "*walk* the talk."

Your decisions must support your cause, not just philosophically, but practically. Assume for a moment that you are an actor. For as long as you can remember, you have watched movies and stage plays with fascination and pictured yourself playing all the lead roles. Growing up, you inspired your siblings to participate in the skits you devised. Your siblings cooperated with your requests, not because acting meant anything to them, but because it meant so much to you.

You won roles in every school play. Whether you played George Washington or John Glenn, you aced the part. You went on to study drama in college and moved to New York City, where you auditioned for every Broadway, off-Broadway, and off-off-Broadway show you could find. Your efforts were rewarded; you got some parts, paid some bills, and began to make a name for yourself.

Then, one opening night, you received a disappointing review. After years of study, you knew reviews were part of the scene. You'd read the life stories. You knew the greats prevailed despite having received bad notices. Yet, a single review thrust you into the emotional basement. Insecurity and rejection overwhelmed you to the degree that you considered quitting your dream and finding a less threatening career.

Imagine that you are facing this choice right now. Clearly, it is a make-or-break point in your journey. What you decide here will determine where you end up. Will you take the reviewer's words in stride and become a better actor and stronger person for it? Or will you allow a blow to your ego to revise your sense of self, tag you with a badge of shame, and rescind your destiny?

Will you consciously cooperate with your unfolding destiny and accept its downside (in this case, professional scrutiny) or will you sacrifice your dream because you fear being judged as an imperfect actor?

The decision is always yours.

Decisions, Decisions

Written into your destiny code is the power to make right choices; therefore, it is crucial that you recognize and understand your code. When you combine understanding with the commitment to cooperate, your decision-making will support your stated goals.

In the scenario of the forlorn actor, a single decision could have been career-ending. But even our smaller, everyday decisions have a cumulative impact. This effect is described by Jean-Marie Gogue, president of the French Deming Association, an organization involved with the study of management theories:

> The result of an accumulation of small decisions in business is so great that sometimes a successful manager's career can be explained by his skilfull [sic] decision making. For example, these may well be the decisions which determine how well the "grand decision" is carried out.[10]

Grand decisions are the ones we tend to remember most. Yet, we learn how to make them by handling small decisions. Big or small, the right decisions always promote progress. Here is how Gogue defines a right decision:

> Since a decision is always preceded by a goal, either stated explicitly or not, our definition is that a right decision is one which helps the decision maker to reach his goal.[11]

You can see the key connection between goals and decision-making. When aligned with your destiny code, the two are inseparable and compatible. Is it possible to make a right decision by accident? Yes, but it rarely happens. Accidental right decisions are virtually *unconscious* decisions. They are one-offs; you cannot rely upon them to occur consistently enough to produce favorable outcomes over the long haul.

According to Gogue there is another stipulation that is critical in this relationship between goals and decisions: the goals that prompt our decisions must be *real* goals. These are goals that harmonize with one another, are untainted by lies (the lies we tell ourselves and others about our goals), and are undisguised by the fear of transparency.[12] Our goals must be *real.*

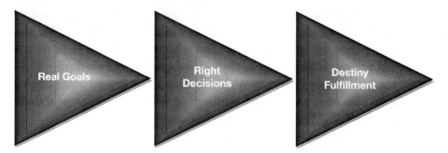

Real goals are what I call *well-formed outcomes*—"the clear and comprehensive expression of a desired future result."[13] My book, *Live Your Dreams,* describes well-formed outcomes at length. For now, suffice to say that a well-formed outcome:

Describes and defines what you want to achieve.

Includes an explanation of why you want to achieve it.

Delineates the terms and conditions under which you want to achieve it and is framed within a realistic life context.

Includes consideration of all suitable approaches, addresses realistic timeframes, and considers whether key factors are in your control.[14]

Stating your well-formed goals according to these standards takes intentionality. This conscious process helps to ensure the quality of your goals. If you think them through to this degree, they are likely to be real goals. With that in mind, Gogue outlines three steps to making right decisions:[15]

The first step is to assess the available actions that can be taken (to achieve your desired results) and the events that will result (from those actions). In the case of the forlorn actor, taking this inventory would have exposed several choices. One would have been to embrace reviews and honor their role in producing better actors.

A second choice would have been to accept the reality of reviews, but deny the value of the negative ones. As with the first choice, the actor would have continued to pursue the acting dream. In this case, however, potentially valuable information would have been ignored, possibly leading to a lesser degree of success over time.

We know that our actor considered chucking his career altogether (a consideration likely made by every actor at some point). This choice would have prevented destiny fulfillment (at least temporarily). The development of the actor's craft would have been arrested and true destiny would have been replaced with a substitute (unless the actor had the courage to override the decision and return to the world of acting with determination, possibly even turning the "near miss" into a new source of motivation).

There are other possible choices and resulting events, but you get the idea of how the first step works.

The second step in arriving at a right decision is to map out the considered actions and resulting events on a "decision tree." This is a diagram or verbal representation that projects the possible outcome of each available action. It also projects the decisions that will need to be made as a result of each action and result. For example: If I choose to quit acting, my acting career will end. When my career ends, I will have to decide what my new vocation will be.

Gogue's decision-making pattern is for businesses. You can simplify the approach to suit your needs. The important thing is to follow your available choices to their logical conclusions and develop a sense of which conclusions are the most likely to occur. Seeing all the options and outcomes play out on paper could have helped our actor diffuse a surge of negative emotions and press on. It would have provided the context needed to evaluate the bad review accurately and assess the spectrum of future risks and rewards.

The third step is to develop a strategy based on the information developed in the previous two steps. The right strategy capitalizes on the right combination of decisions and probable outcomes. In the case of the beleaguered actor, the most benefit would have been gained by (1) continuing to hone the craft of acting and (2) choosing to embrace the reviewer's remarks and use them to advantage—not where short-term feelings are concerned, but where longer-term goals are concerned.

Make every decision for all it is worth. Decisions are not hurdles; they are portals to destiny fulfillment.

Think It Through _____

How good are you at making right decisions? To what degree have you followed the three steps proposed by Jean-Marie Gogue? To what degree are you flying by the seat of your pants and hoping that luck will be on your side?

Avoid Conflicting Goals

Gogue is clear: right decisions can only be framed in the context of *real* goals.[16] Real goals harmonize with one another. Let's return to the realm of acting to see how this works. In this case, we will consider a young woman whose goal it is to become a working actor. A second goal, now fulfilled, is to relocate to New York City in order to audition for stage roles.

Because musical roles are common in theater, this actor might establish a third goal: taking or continuing dance and voice lessons. This goal is compatible with the first two. Do you see how these goals—(1) pursue an acting career (2) move to New York (3) take dance and vocal lessons—work in harmony (no pun intended) to produce the desired result?

The opposite of having harmonized goals is to pursue conflicting goals. Most fledgling actors need to pay the bills while they wait for their big break. Because most auditions are held in the daytime; it makes sense for actors to work during the evening hours—not so late as to be exhausted for early morning auditions, but not so early as to be unavailable.

But what if our second actor dislikes working at night? What if she decides she would rather work in a bank than wait tables in a supper club? If she concedes to this preference, she will almost certainly work during business hours. What then happens to her primary goal? And what becomes of the other goals she has established in support of her pursuit?

It is easy to see that working in a bank conflicts with all the actor's other goals. What is the point of her living in New York City if she cannot attend auditions? How helpful are her dance and vocal lessons if she never gets to use those skills to further her career? It is wonderful to be able to dance and sing well, but she did not take expensive lessons for the privilege of singing in the shower and dancing at friends' weddings.

The actor's conflicting goals are not supporting her dream; they are frustrating her destiny code and professed ambitions. This example of the actor and the banker's job seems like a no-brainer, because the plan is clearly destined to fail. But conflicting goals are not always so clear cut.

Often, the conflict is the internal one we discussed in Chapter 3: the desire for security versus the quest for destiny fulfillment. As goals go, these are in conflict. Destiny fulfillment assumes the taking of risks—often substantial risks. As we have learned, the desire for security is a relentless taskmaster demanding greater and greater levels of self-protection. This conflict can only result in disappointment because it forces us to minimize potential in order to maximize safety (a delusion altogether).

Wasn't that the crux of the matter when a bad review tempted our first actor to quit the business? On the one hand, he risked it all to move to New York and enter a highly competitive field. He knew it was an all-or-nothing proposition; he could become a starving artist or he could hit it big and become a household name. As big a risk as he took, he struggled internally with the fear of rejection. The only way to avoid that risk was to quit the business.

Beware of conflicting goals. They produce destiny paralysis and long-term pain. Be particularly alert to the internal conflicts that often spring from a fear of failure (as in the case of the bad review). Find a mentor who knows the following two things:

1. Failure is the only road to success.
2. Freedom to fail is the only cure for risk aversion.

Honor Destiny Appointments

An important part of conscious cooperation with your destiny code is to honor destiny appointments. You remember Cynthia Rowley's destiny appointment with the Marshall Field buyer on the Chicago El train (see Chapter 4). Once that unexpected meeting took place, the landscape of Rowley's changed. It changed because she cooperated with her destiny code; she recognized the meeting as a destiny appointment and honored it as such.

If right decision-making requires an assessment of available actions and their possible results, then we need to be consciously aware of every destiny appointment that comes our way. Cynthia Rowley could easily have missed her once-in-a-lifetime opportunity. She could have seen her weekend challenge as an insurmountable one. She could have assumed that she was not up to the task because she was "just a student." She might have allowed herself to be overwhelmed by the odds, knowing that only a select group of designers had their collections in the prestigious department store.

In other words, she could have rejected the burden of her destiny and disqualified herself from success.

Critical incidences like this are often missed or dishonored—and often inadvertently. Some pass us by because we fail to pay adequate attention to them. The distractions of pressing issues and problems can look bigger than a seemingly minor opportunity. Remember: Cynthia Rowley's destiny appointment did not happen in a penthouse, but on a crowded commuter train—with another commuter! Not only were the particulars of the meeting mundane, but Rowley was probably over her head in school projects as it was. She had no guarantees that this "chance" occurrence and the weekend blitz would have any long-term value.

Destiny appointments are lost when we don't give ourselves permission to honor them. We may see ourselves as being "too busy" with the "urgent" issues of the present to pause and maximize opportunities for future benefit. Sometimes, we are afraid to believe in our ability to handle the opportunities that come our way. Although it is true that none of us can do everything; each of us can do everything that is tied to our destinies.

Do not be so busy disqualifying yourself that you discredit your capacity to succeed. You were built for success. Everything you need to succeed is already inside of you. Stop, look, and listen. Every destiny appointment has long-term value. And you never know which one will be a game-changer.

Until you honor who you are...until you honor your giftedness...until you honor the destiny appointments in your life, you will find destiny fulfillment to be elusive.

Move Out of Survival Mode

At the core of this chapter is your conscious cooperation with your destiny code. It is within your power to transform your experiences at the bottom into journeys to the top.

Before we close this chapter, we need to revisit another critical choice in the realm of destiny fulfillment. It hearkens back to our discussion in Chapter 5 about choosing our battles. The choice here is between survival mode and the pursuit of destiny. Both are battles; but the battles are not equal. We must become consciously aware of which battle we will choose—and which battle we have chosen by default.

It is here that unspoken goals can be deadlocked in an internal conflict of massive proportions. Whether or not we recognize the presence of the conflict, it will keep us in chains of our own making. For that reason, I'm going to describe it in the starkest possible language. It may sound brutally honest and it is. This is *not* the time to mince words.

Survival mode is an unconscious way of life that robs good, able-bodied, gifted people of hope, prosperity, and fulfillment. Because it is unconscious (and for many other reasons), it is diametrically opposed to destiny achievement. It is a fear-based lifestyle in which the "survivor's" goal is to squeak through each day without losing what little he or she has left.

I told you I wasn't going to mince words. It is my hope that if even a remnant of survival mode lurks in your unconscious mind, it will be revealed and yanked out by its roots. You see, the term *survival mode* is actually a misnomer. This lifestyle is actually a form of death, albeit death by a thousand cuts. Even as your mind envisions your dream with joy, survival mode surreptitiously negates it. It is no wonder that so many leave this earth without enjoying the fulfillment of their dreams.

Survival mode is a type of bunker mentality. Above the bunker, the bullets of life are flying. Rather than risking having your head blown off, you hunker down and wait for the battle to end or a ceasefire to be called. You do the essentials—just what you need to do to get by—and you wait for "another day" when you can "afford to" avail yourself of an opportunity, a day when you believe conditions will be more conducive to a positive outcome. You may be waiting for a day when you feel stronger, look thinner, are better educated, aren't heartbroken or exhausted, or can find the outside help you think you need.

Meanwhile, life is on hold. Every day, you put out prairie fires: you react to emergencies and mishaps and work hard to put everything back where it was before the crisis hit. At times, it feels as though you are actually accomplishing something, especially if nothing else is lost or broken in the process. In reality, you are on the hamster wheel of self-preservation. Your arms and legs are flailing, but you are not going anywhere.

You are making busy while waiting for a break in the battle. The deception of survival mode is that the battle never ends and there are no ceasefires. Destiny is experienced on the battlefield of life—not in the bunker, but up above where the bullets are flying. The battlefield is where you discover that you *can* do it. It is the messy place where you find out what you and all of us are made of—the amazing raw material of destiny achievement.

If you stay in the bunker, resources will remain scarce, fires will continue to flare, and your future will remain uncertain. Postponement will become an habitual unconscious choice. Your dreams and desires will remain buried because you believe your feelings must be ignored for you to survive. This is where short-term relief (a counterfeit of comfort) is exchanged for your real goals. The end result? The loss of long-term pleasure and a life of long-term pain.

The mantra of survival mode is common: "Well, maybe someday, but not today. Right now I've got too many other things to worry about."

Survival mode can become a chronic condition and often does. How many people do you know who are living this way? Has someone in your family chosen this battle? Do you have friends who are struggling under the weight of it? Are *you* stuck in survival mode?

If your answer is *yes* or even *maybe*, I believe you are coming alive—really alive—even as you read these words. Know this—today is the best possible day to dump survival mode and begin living in *conscious cooperation* with your destiny code.

Survival mode can win, but only if you tolerate it. You can resist it by becoming fully conscious and aware of your tendencies. You can become stronger by connecting with the right people. Often, a mentor will interrupt your life and awaken that gut-level yearning inside by modeling what you long for. In an instant, the light goes on and you hear yourself say, "I've got to have that. I must move in that realm. I will not relent until I experience that. What must I do to get there?"

All of a sudden, the yearning within you cannot be quenched, because once you see your destiny, you cannot *unsee* it. Like the miners who lived in the dark for sixty-nine days, you cannot forget your desire to see the sunlight again. Once the yearning comes to the level of your consciousness, your capacity to live in survival mode is forever ruined.

Before you were awakened, you could not see that you were bound in survival mode. But now your dream has come alive in your heart. It's not just a want. It's a deeply felt need—so deep that it hurts. Your destiny desires have been unearthed from layers of rejection, disappointment, and loss. Freedom is calling.

You cannot reenter the bunker. You could not do it even if you tried. A lesser life will no longer do. The constricted place that held you captive in the bowels of the earth is no longer enough. It is too dark, too humid, too confining. Like the Chilean miners set free from their entombment, you will never again be satisfied with two spoons of tuna and a sip of milk. You have tasted the cool fresh air on the surface; you have eaten a good meal; you have tasted the realm of possibility and *nothing* can drive you back under.

You have real goals and a real destiny. You will not be denied.

Download Your Code

1. What, in your opinion, is the meaning of life? What is the meaning of your life?
2. Which area of your life seems to be in chaos? What meaning have you found in the midst of the chaos? How has your destiny code played a part?
3. Describe one way in which you are consciously cooperating with your destiny code. What results have you seen so far (in terms of progress toward goals, increased self-worth, improved clarity of your life's vision, etc.)?
4. How is the development of real goals or the lack thereof affecting the quality of your decision-making? What areas of improvement have you seen? What improvements are still needed?
5. Are there any signs that you are living in survival mode? Explain. How do you think this lifestyle began? How do you feel about it ending?

Notes

1. Jonathan Franklin, "Chilean Miners' Families Pitch Up at Camp Hope," guardian.co.uk, August 25, 2010, http://www.guardian.co.uk/world/2010/aug/25/chilean-miners-families-camp-hope (accessed October 18, 2010).
2. Craig McMurtrie, "Aussie Drill Expert Called to Chile Mine Rescue," ABC News, August 24, 2010, http://www.abc.net.au/news/stories/2010/08/24/2991575.htm?section=world (accessed October 18, 2010).
3. Federico Quilodran, "Dinner for Chile Miners—2 Spoonfuls of Tuna," Associated Press via msnbc.com, August 24, 2010, http://www.msnbc.msn.com/id/38830593/ns/world_news-americas/ (accessed October 18, 2010).
4. Ibid.
5. Mark Chironna, *Seven Secrets to Unfolding Destiny* (Shippensburg, PA: Destiny Image Publishers, 2010), 25.
6. Viktor Frankl, *Man's Search for Meaning* (Boston: Beacon Press, 1992), 105, http://books.google.com/books?id=K2AvZmco3E0C&dq=man's+search+for+meaning+victor+frankl&printsec=frontcover&source=bl&ots=cKnkG1CAgh&sig=EWojeCGMMlXdMUeOoppa8ajTUfY&hl=en&ei=uEFBSrOoH4j2sQPW8tDxCA&sa=X&oi=book_result&ct=result&resnum=5 (accessed October 18, 2010).
7. Chironna, 27.

8. Chironna, 41; Frankl, 86.

9. Chironna, 41.

10. Jean-Marie Gogue, "Improving the Art of Decision Making," The French Deming Association, http://www.fr-deming.org/afed-A1.pdf (accessed October 18, 2010).

11. Ibid.

12. Ibid.

13. Mark J. Chironna, *Live Your Dream* (Shippensburg, PA: Destiny Image Publishers, 2009), 82.

14. Ibid.

15. The following three steps are based on Gogue's article. Jean-Marie Gogue, "Improving the Art of Decision Making," cited above.

16. Ibid.

7
Ride the Rollercoaster

Over the past seven years I had experienced so many highs and lows, and had finally set about facing my fears.

—Michael J. Fox, *Lucky Man*

Destiny codes unfold in as many ways as there are people. Some folks recognize their destiny codes early and rocket straight into realms of fulfillment. Others pack extra trail mix and sort through the signposts on the long and winding road before they bump into the one thing that really makes them tick. Only then are they ready to put their destiny eggs into a single basket.

The story of actor, activist, and author Michael J. Fox is truly one of a kind. As a young man, it was clear that he had many gifts and aspirations. Yet, he focused his energies on the *one thing* at an age when many are preoccupied with hiding their acne from members of the opposite sex.

Like most Canadian kids, Fox loved hockey and dreamed of a career in the National Hockey League. In his teens, his interests expanded. He began experimenting with creative writing and art and played guitar in a succession of rock-and-roll garage bands before ultimately realizing his affinity for acting.[1]

At fifteen, Fox made his professional acting debut on a Canadian sitcom. Three years later, he relocated to Los Angeles. There he won bit parts and soon landed his signature television role as Alex P. Keaton, the business-minded, old-beyond-his-years teenager on the American sitcom, *Family Ties*.[2]

Fox also succeeded on the big screen, perhaps most notably in the *Back to the Future* film series. With the rare ability to switch seamlessly between comedy and drama, television and the silver screen, Fox returned to television in the hit series *Spin City.* It was in that season of his life that Michael's career path took its most unexpected turn.

Steep Curve Ahead

Michael J. Fox's career was humming. *Family Ties* had a long, successful run and Fox remained in demand. All his career indicators pointed upward; the sky was the limit for the beloved actor. Then, while on location in 1990, Fox (who was not yet thirty), awakened to a twitch; his pinkie finger was moving on its own.[3] It was his first clue that something was wrong.

> It would be a year of questions and false answers that would satisfy me for a time, fueling my denial and forestalling the sort of determined investigation that would ultimately provide the answer. That answer came from a doctor who would inform me that I had a progressive, degenerative, and incurable neurological disorder; one that I may have been living with for as long as a decade before suspecting there might be anything wrong. This doctor would also tell that I could probably continue acting for "another ten good years," and he would be right about that, almost to the day. What he did not tell me—what no one could—is that these last ten years of coming to terms with my disease would turn out to be the best ten years of my life—not in spite of my illness but because of it.[4]

Being diagnosed with Parkinson's disease doesn't sound like the "best" of anything. It is a path fraught with challenges, as Fox attests. He compared the physical aspects of the disease to a divorce between brain and mind in which the brain seizes custody of the body.[5] For an actor whose body plays so powerfully into his craft, this loss of control could only be devastating.

Yet, as far as Michael J. Fox is concerned, the best ten years of his life had just begun. In his bestselling book, *Lucky Man,* Fox explains that the person he was prior to Parkinson's is gone. He sees that as a good thing, writing: "I never want to go back to that life—a sheltered, narrow existence fueled by fear and made liveable by insulation, isolation, and self-indulgence."[6]

The trajectory of Fox's life shifted dramatically. The freewheeling, hard-living actor with the world on a string unexpectedly found himself at the end of a short, unforgiving leash. He could choose the life of victimhood; he could immerse himself in denial (which he tried at first); or he could come to grips with the "lost" place to which Parkinson's led. Fox squared his shoulders and faced the facts. He acknowledged the physical degradation and professional uncertainty ahead.

Like Joseph on his way to Egypt, Michael's unexpected change in direction seemed diametrically opposed to his career path. But he held the reins; he would not become a victim, but a lifelong learner whose unexpected education would serve a larger purpose.

Fox entered the path of his tribulation with unanswered questions and a willingness to allow his trial to become his process. Instead of a physically active man with a self-centered point of view, he became a physically challenged man with a heart to give others hope and a better life.

In *Lucky Man,* Fox gives unvarnished accounts of his symptoms and the professional difficulties he faced:

> I can vividly remember all those nights when the studio audience, unknowingly, had to wait for my symptoms to subside. I'd be backstage, lying on my dressing room rug, twisting and rolling around, trying to cajole my neuroreceptors into accepting and processing the L-dopa I so graciously provided. When that approach failed, I'd spruce up the walls with fist-size holes, the graffiti of my frustration. How much longer could this go on?[7]

It took time for Fox to share his plight with fans, but the time came. In order to move forward, he had to let go of the fear of losing his career. Can you imagine the opposing voices begging his attention? *When your fans learn the truth, they'll drop you like a hot potato. When your symptoms take over, your value will be over, too. You'll be washed up before you're forty.*

Fox realized that as long as he kept his condition secret, he could not be free[8] to be himself or to live an integrated, purpose-filled life. He chose self-acceptance and trusted others to accept him as he was—a gifted, valuable human being who happened to have an illness. Fox risked being known and was, therefore, empowered to discover a new path. That new path would prove to be a thing of beauty.

> "...*I have this disease.* This is not a *role* I'm playing. Like any other patient, my participation is uniquely informed by my experience. I know the issues, I'm compelled to understand the science, and I share my community's sense of urgency."[9]
>
> —Michael J. Fox

Face Your Pain

Today, the Michael J. Fox Foundation for Parkinson's Research is able to raise awareness and funding at a high level. Because Fox is well-known and chose to be visible during his struggle, he has "sparked a national conversation about Parkinson's disease."[10] According to Fox, Parkinson's patients are best equipped to create awareness, because they live the reality. His celebrity is what Fox describes as "useful currency." To his credit, he has "discovered a wonderful way to spend it."[11]

His enormous impact notwithstanding, Fox has paid a high price. Like anyone who has experienced a trial of this magnitude, he has experienced real pain—not just physically, but emotionally, professionally, and perhaps in other ways. As is true of all destiny achievers, it is in the midst of pain that his glorious destiny continues to unfold.

In Chapter 6, we touched briefly on the benefits of dealing with pain rather than burying it. Wounds must be exposed to the air if they are to heal. Without healing, destiny fulfillment is hindered, in part because buried pain diminishes your ability to live consciously. It causes you to mask your feelings, suppress your emotions, and deny yourself resolution and closure. Burial doesn't kill pain; it institutionalizes it!

There are times when you must compartmentalize your emotions. When Captain Chelsey Sullenberger faced engine failure aboard Flight 1549, he had to set his emotions aside and deal with the emergency at hand. He had to take a clinical view of the facts, manage his thought momentum, and find a reason-based solution to the crisis.

In fight-or-flight moments, you have to push past your feelings in order to survive. But when the emergency is over, you have to face the rollercoaster of emotions in order to heal. Burials are for the dead, not the living. Feelings serve important functions. They give expression to what we find meaningful and moving. They are the outward display of what is in our hearts. They help us to connect with others. They motivate us to take action. They alert us when something is wrong. Feelings are valuable and *human*. They are the bridge between the conscious and unconscious mind.

If we knock out the bridge in order to avoid pain, we become internally disconnected and, therefore, sick. Instead of being healed, we are forced to work—usually in unconscious ways—to keep the simmering pot of hidden pain from boiling over. Having stuffed the original issue, we must stuff every subsequent ache that is triggered deep within us. We end up reacting to situations and people in inappropriate and damaging ways, unable to explain even to ourselves the reasons for our reactions.

Buried pain produces a continuum of maladjustment: fear brings pain; pain fosters shame; shame breeds anger; anger promotes vengeance. Can you see how opposite this is to healing? Can you imagine the exponential increase of pain that is caused when we try to bury, rather than acknowledge, our emotions?

Think It Through _____

How do you handle painful emotions and experiences? How strong is the bridge between your conscious and unconscious mind? How might it be strengthened?

Find Those Buried Bones

Let's take a closer look the effects of buried pain and the unhealthy progression it produces. The process begins with the onset of a painful event or experience and involves our decisions about whether or not to deal with pain in productive ways. If we choose, even unconsciously, to suppress our pain, we create a destructive chain of emotional events:

Fear— Whether we are talking about Joseph at the point of his brothers' betrayal, or someone receiving a diagnosis of a catastrophic illness, the decision to bury pain will cause fear to become a constant companion. No matter how hard we try to deny it, we know when there are unresolved issues lurking within us. Instead of tackling the original issue, we live under the canopy of a nameless, secondary fear—the fear that the buried secret will rise to the surface someday.

Everyone experiences unhealthy fears. These fears anchor themselves at the level of conscious awareness. Yet over time, they foster unconscious reactions and build invisible walls around us. Fear paralyzes our capabilities and stifles advancement. Left unchallenged, fear steals purpose and silences our voices. It leave us in vegetative states, emotionally speaking.

Pain—Remember that feelings are the bridge between the conscious and unconscious mind. Pain attacks our feelings by numbing them, thereby severing this vital connection. Pain is the underpinning of fear; it continues to generate new and evolving fears which, in turn, generate more pain. If the initial response to pain is to bury it, the pain becomes more widespread, and therefore more threatening, demanding more burials. Unresolved pain will produce a vicious cycle of trigger…response…trigger.

Shame—Pain underlies fear and shame underlies pain. We work hard to bury pain because we know that something is wrong. The problem is that we misunderstand the issue. Instead of affirming that *something is wrong,* we assume that something is wrong *with us.* One of the starkest examples of this kind of shame is seen in those who are abused. Victims of abuse eventually hold themselves responsible for the terrible acts of their abusers. Often, the abused believe that they deserve to be abused. Shame literally steals identity.

Anger—Even when we think that we deserve our pain, we are angered by injustice. When we choose to bury pain and the shame we have attached to it, we have no healthy way to dispose of the anger caused by the offenses we suffer.

Anger is always symptomatic of fear and is an outgrowth of pain. We become angry when we fear that we have lost control or when we believe that someone is using, abusing, or slandering us. Anger creates sickness. It destroys relationships and kills potential. To bury or ignore anger is costly—it only becomes more virulent and more costly to relationships and destiny outcomes.

You may know someone with an anger problem. If you have known them for any length of time, you have no doubt seen the damage anger has done in the areas of professional advancement and family relations.

Vengeance—When pain is buried, the path to healing is buried, too. Without some way out of pain's prison, getting even becomes the only viable source of relief. Instead of dealing with the original issue (an offense, event, attitude, or misunderstanding), we seek solace by thinking, "I'll show them. They think I won't make it, but I'll prove that I can make it." You might not even want to retaliate, but the pressure to prove yourself becomes overwhelming.

Vengeance is not a viable solution. Nor does it fix anybody else's wagon. Vengeance destroys the avenger. It hardens the heart, saps energy, distorts relationships, and destroys futures. Taken to the extreme, vengeance can be deadly, as any local newscast will attest.

Buried pain will take you places you don't want to go. The good news is that there is an alternative, a much sweeter river that you can choose to navigate. Underneath layers of self-protection there is a river of love that wants to flow. It is a river that produces healthy desires that lead in the direction of destiny fulfillment. Your destiny codes cannot function except through love and desire.

More about this later; first let's find a positive way to deal with pain.

Leverage Your Adversity

There is an axiom that says, "What doesn't kill you makes you stronger." There is some truth in this statement; however, I would revise it by adding two qualifiers: "What doesn't kill you will make you stronger *if* you find the context of the difficulty within your destiny code, and *if* you leverage your adversity to produce benefit."

Unless you maintain your sense of purpose and find meaning in the midst of your trials, the ones that don't kill you will make you weaker. Eventually, they will wear you down.

So how do you leverage your adversity? You start with your destiny code in mind; then you make an honest assessment of the pain you are experiencing— but you do all of this in the light of your life's vision.

Simply put, you must acknowledge your difficulties without losing sight of your destiny. For Michael J. Fox (who already possessed the mindset of a destiny achiever), there had to be a season of grieving. Fox had to reckon with the loss of physical wholeness, the effects on family, the disruption to set goals and expectations, the demise of the carefree life (relatively speaking) of a young man at the top of his game.

If you have ever experienced a reversal of fortune, you know that it is like hitting a brick wall without brakes or an airbag. When you realize that the impact has not killed you, you begin to juggle scores of questions. *How can I fix this? What can be saved? How will I make it? What will happen to my family? What will become of my independence…my earning power…my future dreams?…What if?… How?…When?…*

Suddenly, everything you have believed and planned is in jeopardy. You clutch the people and things you treasure; you experience regret for all that you took for granted. This is a deeply emotional and meaningful pivot point on your destiny path. Unless you take the facts of your situation at face value and then dig deeper to determine what you stand to lose, you cannot make even the simplest of quality decisions. Instead, the swift current of adversity will sweep you downstream where you will live powerless and at its whim.

> **Leverage adversity by making an honest assessment of the pain you are experiencing — but do it in the light of your life's vision.**

Next, because you see your situation in light of your destiny codes, you begin to realize that even an unexpected situation is not a rabbit trail, but a kind of destiny appointment to be honored. You may not understand the symbols and signals being displayed, but you know that woven into every circumstance is an essential thread of your destiny fulfillment.

Know this: There are destiny appointments from which you will want to be healed and delivered. They feel wrong, they cause pain, and they strip away your sense of comfort. The only way you can get the healing you desire is to honor these incidents as destiny appointments, even before you fully understand them. Allow them to unfold. Do this not as a bystander, but as an active participant who is watching and learning and empowered to choose new actions. You might not be sure where your choices will lead, but because you are confident that you have a destiny, you know that even your crisis is an opportunity to grow.

When you honor life's difficulties as destiny appointments, you cannot be strangled by the fear of loss. Instead, you look eagerly for the symbols and signals of your destiny code, knowing they will reveal what you stand to gain. Even if you have suffered rejection and loss, you understand that the people and circumstances involved served a larger purpose: they brought you to the place you needed to be, even if it was not a place you would have chosen for yourself.

Uncomfortable destiny appointments are tied to significant others and significant emotional events. They serve—if approached from the perspective of destiny fulfillment—to weave the fabric of your life and relationships more tightly. You discover that you are not in a battle against people, but against bitterness and complacency. You quit trying to fight off the emotional pain; instead you use it to leverage yourself into a new place of personal power.

This is what happened to Joseph. Having acknowledged the intense emotional pain he endured, he was able to say, "My brothers abused and rejected me. Yet, if they hadn't rejected me, I would never have reached my place of destiny: I would not have been in a position to save them and others from starvation."

Michael J. Fox also saw value in the pain he suffered and even described his illness as a gift.[12] Clearly, this perspective is not to be taken lightly, as Fox explains:

> Coping with the relentless assault and the accumulating damage is not easy. Nobody would ever choose to have this visited upon them. Still, this unexpected crisis forced a fundamental life decision: adopt a siege mentality—or embark upon a journey. Whatever it was—courage? acceptance? wisdom?—that finally allowed me to go down the second road (after spending a few disastrous years on the first) was unquestionably a gift—and absent this neurophysiological catastrophe, I would never have opened it, or been so profoundly enriched. That's why I consider myself a lucky man.[13]

For a young actor, the battle with Parkinson's must have looked like the cruelest of rabbit trails. Yet, Michael J. Fox dug deeper and found real meaning in his difficult experience.

> **Leverage adversity by realizing that your situation is not a rabbit trail, but a kind of destiny appointment to be honored.**

Once you decide that you will not drown in life's deep end, you can leverage adversity by focusing and drawing upon your strengths. In seasons of distress and testing, we grow by using our assets. Often they are intangibles, such as optimism or a sense of humor. Other strengths have a more practical side; these include the ability to organize or establish a business plan.

Another strength that is useful in times of difficulty revolves around your vision. There is power in trusting your vision in good times and bad. Like Joseph's dreams of leadership, your destiny vision provides a steady reference point on which you can focus when your ship of life is tossed by rough seas. When doubts arise and despair tries to settle in your heart, your vision becomes your lifeline. Use it to pull your thoughts out of the bad days and into the better days that are ahead. When the signs on the ground point every which way, your vision will always point straight ahead.

Draw upon your strengths and you will grow stronger through every destiny appointment.

> **Leverage adversity by focusing and drawing upon your strengths.**

Another aspect of leveraging your adversity is to discover or see more clearly the *one thing* that makes you tick. Earlier in this chapter, I mentioned those who wander life's trail and bump into the *one thing*. Sometimes, the collision is far more violent, as it was in Joseph's case. The *one thing* to which I refer is your *unique factor*.

> When you recognize it, it will shed new light on your destiny code so that you can read it clearly and live the life you were created to live. Your unique factor is an integral part of you, always available and ready to be activated by you. At this very moment, your unique factor is resident within you. It is either being expressed or is awaiting expression in and through your life.
>
> Your unique factor doesn't always look the way you'd like it to look.... Your unique factor is often the very thing to which you would prefer not to draw attention. What makes us unique can also cause us to feel as though we were sticking out from the crowd.
>
> Yet, the significance of your unique factor demands that you come to terms with it one way or the other.[14]

Remember that Joseph got into trouble with his brothers, in large part because he shared the dreams he'd had in which his family and celestial bodies bowed down to him.

While these dreams were part of Joseph's destiny code, his ability to interpret them was his unique factor. As we will see in a future chapter, it would prove to be his ticket out of slavery. At first, Joseph may well have regretted exposing his unique factor to his brothers. It did, after all, cost him dearly. You may feel the same way about your unique factor. But before you pass judgment, let's examine this aspect of leveraging adversity more closely.

> **Leverage adversity by discovering, or seeing more clearly, the *one thing* that makes you tick—your unique factor.**

Think It Through _____

Whether or not you are in a season of adversity, your unique factor is already resident with you. Do you know what it is? Are you comfortable with it or do you try to keep it under wraps? If you're not sure what it is yet, are you ready to discover it?

Your Unique Factor

Your unique factor is at the core of your destiny code. Just as your destiny is your identity, your unique factor is part of you. It is a constant in your life. Cynthia Rowley's story demonstrates this fact. Remember that she created her first dress when she was just seven years old and is working in the design field to this day.

When you become consciously aware of your unique factor, your sense of self-worth is elevated. All of your other capabilities begin to converge and make sense. They might not have seemed important before your unique factor was revealed; they were just things you did. Now, you seem them in the context of your unique factor and the pieces of your life's puzzle fall into place.

The discovery of your unique factor is an essential for destiny fulfillment. While your unique factor helps you to understand your identity and purpose, it also unlocks your kernel of power. You suddenly realize your capacity to accomplish great things. This knowledge in turn generates a reliable source of motivation. Not only that, but because you understand your unique factor, you become more fluent in the language of your destiny code.

Identifying your unique factor helps you to live from the inside out. Instead of being driven by externals, you are motivated from within by your purpose and the knowledge that you can accomplish it. Awareness and acceptance of your unique factor solidifies the reality of your destiny code. It is no longer a gossamer thread revealed only in rare moments of revelation. Instead, it is tangible link between who you are and what you were born to do.

You cannot deny your unique factor. You either love to sing or you don't. You either have a passion for skiing or you don't. You cannot refute the fact that medical school invigorates you or the sight of a blank canvas stirs your imagination. Your unique factor is part of the internal generator that acts as both compass and energy source. It keeps you pedaling even when the path leads straight up steep hill.

Whatever it is, your *one thing* can also be a source of irritation. Do you remember the Smothers Brothers? Tommy Smothers played the part of the spaced out sibling who was slow to respond and quick to misunderstand. When his serious-minded brother, Dick, would try to set the record straight, Tommy would cock his head and say nothing for a time. His hesitation added to the comedic value of the skit. The routines were hilarious; it was virtually impossible not to laugh at Tommy's perplexed look.

You might be surprised to learn that Tommy's rare comedic gift was partly the result of a learning disability, as Tommy's explains:

> I first realized I was funny in about the fourth or fifth grade. I was dyslexic and I had no idea what that was. I was always the last one to get the spelling thing—the dumb one. I always played that, pretending I was stupid. The thing about being dyslexic, I also have to search for words—it's not just reading. I think of things and words don't come. I never did stutter, but there were these little lapses. It was a gift as far as comedy timing was concerned.[15]

Often, we despise the very thing that can bring us to greatness. It is doubtful that Tommy Smothers wanted to be known for his lapses, especially during childhood, when fitting in is so important. Likewise, the uniqueness of your unique factor may be the one thing you don't want to deal with. It may have brought you pain or embarrassment when all you really wanted was to fit in with the crowd.

Often, we fail to honor our unique factor because it seems so common to us. Has anyone ever pointed out an area of your giftedness that you took for granted? You might have assumed that it was the same piece of "equipment" everyone else had—but it wasn't. Or you might have seen it as different, but inconsequential.

Your unique factor is unique. The statement is redundant, but it needs to be. You have something inside that no one else has, and when you consciously honor it, the sky truly is the limit. Honoring your unique factor will create the chain of events, relationships, and opportunities that are authentic parts of your destiny code. You will find yourself favored by others. You will experience increase. You will tap into previously untapped potential so that all of your capabilities find a place to flourish.

Let me warn you that, until you discover your unique factor, you will find yourself doing many things that fail to form a cohesive whole. You might even subconsciously avoid the one thing because it seems to create conflict. Have you been there? You excel in science class; your friends deride you and call you "teacher's pet." You excel at work, your boss puts you on the fast track to promotion, and your best friend becomes aloof or sarcastic. You begin to prosper and your favorite neighbor quits inviting your kids to his kids' birthday parties.

Do you see how full engagement with the *one thing* can seem threatening? We *say* we want it all, yet we fear having it all. We become used to our discomforts. If we are not attentive and accountable to our destiny codes, we become accustomed to lack and dissatisfaction. Somewhere hidden deep in our insecurities is the sense that having it all will require us to change. Although we might be praying night and day for our circumstances to change, we might not want to change ourselves.

It is not surprising that we often avoid dealing with our unique factor until we find ourselves in periods of crisis and isolation. When we are alone with our "stuff"; when we have exhausted our own methods; when we are at our wits' end; the *one thing* rises to the surface—and we cannot ignore it any longer. Like Joseph, we find that the very thing that has gotten us into trouble before is really the key to our destiny.

A Tale of Two Wars

In Chapter 5, we talked about choosing your battle. We discussed the fact that life involves warfare. We can fight unending battles for survival or we can fight for the fullness of destiny. Choosing the latter does not mean an end to warfare. Often, it is just the beginning of a war you never expected to wage.

Once you settle the issue of your pain; once you realize that your unique factor is an asset rather than a liability; once you earnestly buy into your destiny code; you will likely hit some headwinds. Here you must be aware of two wars: the first is the good fight that is based in honest love for others and the desire to fulfill a beneficial destiny; the second is a war you enter at the beck and call of others.

The latter war involves the forces of *envy, revenge, temptation,* and *ingratitude.* Unless you guard your heart and focus on your purpose, you will find yourself swept up in this war like a like a small stone carried by a rushing river. You might even believe you belong there, fighting the forces of nature. In reality, you have a choice: you can rise above this war or you can set up house in trenches you were never called to inhabit.

This war begins when your destiny pursuit causes others to act out their insecurities. You may have commiserated with them before. You may have shared the poverty battle or a season in the lost place, but now your destiny code is unfolding before their eyes. Your unique factor is producing fruit in your life and in the lives of others. Your vocabulary is changing. There's a new skip in your step that expresses a new determination to run the destiny race with everything you've got.

People in high places are showing you favor and opening ever greater doors of opportunity. You lived in obscurity before, but now your name is out there. There's a buzz on the street. You are moving into new circles. People who know you say,

"Have you seen So-and-so lately? Have you heard what's going on in her life?" or, "Did you meet his new wife?" "Did you hear about her new business?"

Those who knew you back when will understand that you have advanced beyond the lost place. They catch glimpses of you living among the "found" ones.

Even if you have only taken a couple of baby steps, they can see that you are advancing while they are standing still.

Isn't that what happened to Joseph? He told his brothers his dreams.[16] They could easily have blown off the dreams—they just looked like fantasies, after all. It was not as though anyone in the neighborhood had yet bowed down to Joseph. There were no media camped outside the family home and no fans screaming Joseph's praises. Joseph was, on the face of it, Daddy's pet and a kid brother with an active imagination.

Perhaps the brothers recognized an unspoken *something*. We can see from their actions that they felt terribly threatened by the teenager. They went to awful lengths to rid themselves of him and rid him of his destiny. Their emotions were so out of control that they found it in their hearts to jeopardize Joseph's life and break their father's heart.

Have you ever been broadsided by those you loved and trusted? Was it because of something you did or because of who you are?

When you allow your destiny code to detected by others; when you are free to celebrate your giftedness, not by boasting, but by living it; when you have been proven at some level, whether in your integrity or your tenacity; when you are ready to move into another dimension of your destiny—the first headwind you hit will be *envy.*

---

en·vy

noun

1: painful or resentful awareness of an advantage enjoyed by another joined with a desire to possess the same advantage[17]

When you are envious, it is more than a sense of disappointment that somebody else was chosen instead of you. Envy manifests in a variety of ways. Some people act out their envy in a passive-aggressive war dance. They lash out, not by telling you how envious they are, but by withholding love, affirmation, or support. Others display their envy outright with cutting words or hurtful actions.

---

re·venge

noun

1: a desire for revenge…
2: an act or instance of retaliating in order to get even…
3: an opportunity for mgetting satisfaction…[18]

Envy can lead to an even more serious consequence: *revenge.* Yes. Some people will feel so driven by envy that they will seek to take you out. Somewhere deep in their unconscious minds, they know that if they can prevent you from having something (recognition, reward, prosperity, promotion, favor), they can justify not having it themselves.

Revenge is often seen in the workplace in the form of damaging rumors or project sabotage. Sometimes a supervisor who feels threatened by your gifting will attempt to hinder your progress out of fear that you might become her boss someday.

Sometimes, the vengeful choose to "erase" those they envy. Have you ever had a good friend distance himself for no apparent reason? It might have been a convenient way to avoid having to deal with you. This form of revenge supports denial: envious individuals believe that if they don't see your progress; they won't have to face their stagnation, either.

This war is a test of your integrity and vision. You can allow the envy of others to derail you. You can allow their approval to be more important than your destiny achievement. It would be a foolish choice, but not an unusual one. Rejection is unpleasant. If you allow your emotions to drive you, you will avoid rejection at all cost. Without realizing it, you will empower others to take you out.

---

temp·ta·tion

noun

1: the act of tempting or the state of being tempted especially to evil : enticement
2: something tempting : a cause or occasion of enticement[19]

The third headwind you will face is *temptation.* Believe it or not, the greatest challenges do not come in times of failure; they come during the days of success. The more power you have through the unfolding of your destiny, the more freedom you have in the form of choices, opportunities, access, and influence. This is the place where your integrity will be most severely tested.

You have no doubt heard heartrending stories of successful men and women who experienced moral and ethical failures in horribly public ways. Politicians, professional athletes, celebrities, and even clergy are caught off guard by temptation. Often, the successful unfolding of destiny deludes people. If they are not morally and spiritually grounded, they believe they are bulletproof. Offers of temporary pleasure abound, while the reality of long-term pain seems remote.

If you allow integrity to guide you, you will resist short-term temptation and enjoy the intended long-term pleasures of destiny fulfillment. Either way, you must choose.

---

in·grat·i·tude

noun

forgetfulness of or poor return for kindness received : ungratefulness[20]

The fourth element in this war is *ingratitude*. Even when you do what is right and good, some will find fault or reject you. If your character is weak or if insecurity drives an overwrought need for affirmation, this ingratitude can throw you off course.

There is another side of ingratitude. It involves the failure to recognize the pure beauty of your destiny. If you seek only what others can do for you; if you see every situation as an opportunity to profit or compete; you will ultimately forfeit your destiny. You might experience financial and worldly success, yet you will not reach the heights of favor, honor, respect, or accomplishment for which you were destined.

The Good War

Woven into your destiny fulfillment is a good war. It is a fight for the forces of love and desire and all that issues forth from them. This love runs deep; it is the love of others above yourself. It produces desires that are neither superficial nor clawing. When you are motivated by love, you desire to act in the best interests of life's biggest and best picture.

This war demands high standards; therefore, many people shrink from it. It is a war that requires vigilance and intentionality. It is won by those who are willing to pay the price for their dreams. It is not for the faint of heart or for those who embrace an entitlement mentality. It is for those who are willing to withstand and leverage adversity. It is for those who are willing to get their hands dirty. It is for those who will not be satisfied to live in mediocrity.

The strategy of the good war is simple. Executing the strategy is hard. It means following your highest desires—to do good…to be merciful…to mentor others…to give aid…to find solutions…to bring comfort…to meet needs. These desires are based in love. This is not romantic love or the love that satisfies your senses. This is a love based in the belief that this life is bigger than you; it is a love that recognizes the inherent and eternal value of people.

When Michael J. Fox was stricken with Parkinson's disease, he could easily have focused his energy, wealth, and other capacities on his own needs. He had suffered a formidable setback. It would have been easy to retreat. He could have circled the wagons and withdrawn from the public eye. Nobody would have blamed him for doing it.

But Fox recognized that this life is bigger than any one person's struggle. Having borne the burden of Parkinson's, he was all too aware of the needs, hopes, and dreams of others. His setback revealed a new mission and he accepted the call. He understood that he was uniquely qualified to be part of the solution for millions of Parkinson's patients around the world.

Even if you disagree with elements of Fox's strategy to conquer Parkinson's, you must honor his commitment. His new mission was in his destiny code. It was revealed in a time of great difficulty, but once Fox grasped it, he began directing his energy and resources in ways that cooperated with his code. He used his power to network with others; he devised methods by which to accomplish his goals. The love and desire that motivated him caused him to recognize the grand design of everything that had already happened in his life and all that was yet to occur. He embraced the symbols and signals of his destiny code and he leveraged his adversity. He focused, not on naysayers or obstacles, but on the cause.

He chose to fight the good war. So can you—even when life is a rollercoaster.

Download Your Code

1. Is there an experience that divided your life into *before* and *after?* Explain and describe how the person you became *after* differed from the person you were *before.*
2. Describe a situation in which you had to first manage your thought momentum and then return to face the pain. Are there any situations where the order of these responses was reversed or incomplete? What corrections can you make now?
3. Have you buried any "bones" of shame or anger? Explain.
4. Choose an area of adversity and consider it in light of the four steps to leveraging adversity. What are the first two actions you will take to use this adversity to serve your purpose?
5. Which of the two wars do you fight most often? Is there room for improvement? How does "the good war" enhance your perspective of your destiny pursuit?

Notes

1. "About Michael," Michael J. Fox Foundation for Parkinson's Research, http://www.michaeljfox.org/about_aboutMichael.cfm. "About Michael," (accessed 10/16/10).
2. Ibid.
3. Michael J. Fox, *Lucky Man* (New York: Hyperion, 2002), 2.
4. Ibid., 4-5
5. Ibid., 4.
6. Ibid., 6.
7. Ibid., 223.
8. Ibid.

9. Ibid., 252.

10. Ibid, 228.

11. Ibid. 252.

12. Ibid., 5.

13. Ibid.

14. Dr. Mark J. Chironna, *Live Your Dream* (Shippensburg, PA: Destiny Image Publishers, 2009), 36.

15. "Famous People Who Are Dislexic Or Had Dislexia," Disabled World, http://www.disabled-world.com/artman/publish/article_2130.shtml#ixzz 12Z9CIcj7 (accessed October 22, 2010).

16. The details of Joseph's story as noted in this chapter are taken from the Book of Genesis, chapter 37.

17. Merriam-Webster Online Dictionary 2010, s.v. "envy," http://www. merriam-webster.com/dictionary/envy (October 23, 2010).

18. Ibid., s.v. "revenge," http://www.merriam-webster.com/dictionary/revenge? show=1&t=1287962159 (October 24, 2010).

19. Ibid., s.v. "temptation," http://www.merriam-webster.com/dictionary/ temptation (October 24, 2010).

20. Ibid., s.v. "ingratitude," http://www.merriam-webster.com/dictionary/ingratitude (accessed October 24, 2010).

8
Heavyweight in Training

Somehow, I knew that if I were going to survive, I could not become bitter.
I would have to love even those who could not give it in return.

—Muhammad Ali, *The Soul of a Butterfly*

H e grew up amid the harsh reality of segregation, an African-American who tasted the bitterness of society's ills from his earliest years. He was among the millions barricaded on the margins of American life by signs that bluntly ordered: "Whites Only."

Yet, despite the barriers set before him, Cassius Marcellus Clay, Jr. was destined to succeed. As a young man, he would penetrate the American psyche and the nation's lore. Beloved by people of all races, he would be known as "The Greatest." In the world of professional boxing, the title was without dispute; he was indeed, *The Greatest.*

Clay's amazing career began inauspiciously, as great lives often do. He was drawn into boxing in 1954 when somebody stole his Schwinn bicycle, a prized possession for any twelve-year-old lucky enough to own one. Clay was devastated by the loss; he knew the chances of his parents' replacing the stolen bike were slim. He was devastated by the loss, but would not take it sitting down. Clay was determined to find the boy who'd stolen his Schwinn and beat him up.[1]

Clay said as much to policeman Joe Martin, who responded, "You thinking about beating somebody up, you had better learn to fight."[2]

Martin taught boxing skills to local boys and immediately took Clay under his wing. The officer was not particularly impressed by the boy's boxing ability. However, he recognized Clay's fierce determination and self-discipline. The young man showed up on time all the time and trained faithfully, six days a week.[3]

103

By the time Clay was a sophomore in high school, the Schwinn was long gone. But Clay's perseverance had led him to a new and bigger dream: to compete in the Olympics:

> Clay wasn't heavy enough in 1960 to enter the Olympics as a heavyweight. Instead, he was entered in the 178-pound light heavyweight division. He won his first three fights fairly easily. Clay had trained hard for the Olympics. Even in the Olympic village he stayed up late at night to shadowbox in his room while his boxing teammates slept....But his fourth fight proved difficult....Clay came out in the third and final round with the determination that was to become his trademark. He used every bit of the skill and nerve he had to take control of the fight. The end of round three left [his opponent] battered and helpless against the ropes.[4]

Cassius Clay, Jr. overcame every obstacle and found his place on the world stage. The gold-medal winner stood on the Olympic platform with head held high as the stirring notes of "The Star-Spangled Banner" played.

Clay's life—and the boxing world—would never be the same.

Think It Through _____

Think back to a goal you set, but never achieved. Does the determination of young Muhammad Ali provide any insight into your shortfall? How can his approach provide guidance for a current pursuit?

Celebrated and Segregated

From boyhood, Clay had borne the weight of racial discrimination. It affected even the mundane aspects of his life and challenged him to develop a strong sense of identity. In *The Soul of a Butterfly*, the autobiography he wrote with his daughter, Hana Yasmeen Ali, he describes how segregation forced African-American children to contend with grown-up issues of great magnitude:

> One of my first encounters with prejudice happened when I was too young to remember, but I've heard my mother tell the story. She and I were standing at a bus stop. It was a hot day and I was thirsty, so we walked up the block to a small diner, where she asked if she could have a cup of water for her son. The man said he could not help us and closed the door in our faces. I can only imagine the pain my mother felt when she tried to find the words to explain why the man would not give me a glass of water. Even during these times my mother would say, "Hating is wrong, no matter who does the hating. It's just plain wrong."[5]

When Clay was eighteen, Olympic gold dangled from a ribbon around his neck. There was no higher prize and Clay thought the medal would change everything. He was the toast of Louisville and had landed himself a position in the ranks of elite athletes. He had fought for his dream and won. He captured the ultimate athletic prize for his nation. Yet his achievement was not enough to dissolve the steel veil of racial prejudice. Still soaring on the wings of his victory, Clay and a friend were denied service at a Louisville eatery:

> I was sure they were finally going to let me eat downtown. In those days almost every restaurant, hotel, and movie theater in Louisville and the entire South was either closed to Blacks, or had segregated sections. But I thought that my medal would open them up to me.[6]

Clay, who later converted to Islam and changed his name to Muhammad Ali, inhabited a world of contradictions. As an athlete, he was celebrated; as a human being he was dishonored and denied even basic rights. It was a bitter pill for the champion to swallow.

As profound as the disappointment was, Clay was determined to reach higher and continue to excel in boxing and life. He learned to navigate the seemingly irreparable schism between his destiny and cultural environment. From his days as a professional boxer to his current retirement years, his dignity attests to his spirit of excellence. Muhammad Ali became known as "The Greatest" in spite of the difficulties, and perhaps in part, because of them.

Man With a Mission

The firebrand boxer and often controversial figure has made a mark on society that reaches far beyond his exploits in the ring. Muhammad Ali continues to inspire. Countless Americans who witnessed his irrepressible rise to the top—people of all races and creeds—found the courage to pursue their dreams without apology or fear because they saw Ali do it. Even in the days when his outspoken political views stirred angst and contention, his far-reaching influence was acknowledged by all.

Especially in his heyday, Muhammad Ali was a touchstone of destiny fulfillment, and he knew it. Fame had laid upon him a tall order, but Ali never shied away from it. He willingly and thoughtfully bore his unique destiny burden. In 2004, after decades of fame and reflection, Ali wrote about his mission in life—both the one he once thought was his and the one he later recognized as his true calling:

> I thought my purpose was to be that hero who showed children that Black is beautiful. I thought my person was to be that champion who showed White people they couldn't treat Blacks like second-class citizens. I learned that all of these accomplishments were important, but even more important, I gained a platform

that allowed me to carry out my real mission, which has been to encourage all people to respect each other and to live in peace. I am still discovering God's purpose for me.[7]

Quintessential lifelong learner Muhammad Ali has pursued his purpose with poise and enthusiasm. Even now, as he suffers the physical impairments of Parkinson's disease, Muhammad Ali remains the bright, witty, gentle giant who reminds us that destiny fulfillment is achievable, no matter the obstacles.

It is important for each of us to figure out why we were put here on earth by God. The importance of life is to accomplish the task we were given. Without working on this task, life is meaningless Human beings have a basic need and desire to accomplish something before they die—to make a difference.[8]

—Muhammad Ali

Training for Destiny

In his boxing days, Muhammad Ali was known for one-liners and poems that touted his greatness and irritated his opponents. He described himself in the most colorful terms as one who "floats like a butterfly and stings like a bee." He bragged somewhat facetiously about being able to flick the light switch and climb into bed before the room got dark.

Muhammad Ali made what many saw as arrogant claims. Yet, his words were never hollow. He brought the goods to the ring. He was quicker, fitter, and smarter than most anybody in the game. It took time for the boxing establishment to recognize just how good he was; but they found out soon enough.

The great knockout specialist, Sonny Liston, learned about Cassius Clay the hard way. Liston underestimated Clay's ability, as did many at the weigh-in for their historic bout. Clay seemed emotionally out of control. His behavior was like nothing anyone had ever seen from a fighter. Liston thought the upstart was crazy or terrified, or both.[9]

What Liston failed to understand was the degree of Clay's readiness. Clay was prepared to give the champion a shellacking and upset the boxing world in the process. Clay's years of discipline and systematic training had produced a fighter seasoned beyond his years. His mannerisms baffled his competitor, but Clay was essentially "a hard-working guy [who] knew that nothing came easy. Yes, he talked a big game, but boy, did he back it up with his effort in the gym and in the ring."[10]

Months earlier, Liston and Clay had a confrontation in a casino. Clay heckled the champion and Liston put him in his place. Liston was confident that he'd shown the young loudmouth who was boss.[11] But when the two men entered the ring in 1964, the tables turned. Liston was accustomed to knocking out his opponents early, but Clay forced him to fight six punishing rounds, after which Liston's only choice was to surrender.[12]

After Liston went down, it was hard to see Clay's antics as child's play. Clay had proven himself as a force to be reckoned with. He earned his bragging rights; he paid the price every day before he entered the ring. He used everything to his advantage, even the shackles with which society tried to restrain him: He rose above the deep frustration of a hostile, racially-charged environment and, by example, became part of the solution. He broke through the deep limitation that was the 1950s life of a black child in Louisville, Kentucky. He dealt with the pain of the deep emotional and spiritual conflict caused by the injustice he experienced.

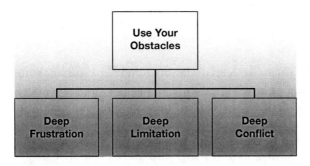

Cassius Clay found a way to use the obstacles. They became barbells in the training room of his life. He used every one of them to his advantage—even the theft of his Schwinn.

Expand Your Capacity

What is true for Muhammad Ali is true for the rest of us: we were born with a sense of destiny lodged in our hearts. This inborn recognition, whether spoken or unspoken, drives our conclusions regarding our progress in life. When dissatisfaction nips at our heels, our destiny codes are speaking. We are programmed to chafe at mediocrity. Therefore, our bouts of dissatisfaction are noteworthy and must be examined.

Are you living with a generalized sense of frustration? Do you feel trapped in your job or your neighborhood? Are you trying to blow off your frustration because you believe relief is unavailable? Are you sure you have correctly identified the source of it?

These are important questions to answer. Too often, we accept frustration as though it were an unknown and incurable disease. In reality, we can both identify the disease and eliminate the symptoms. The first step is self-examination.

Ask yourself whether your job or your neighborhood (or whatever you believe is causing your frustration) is really at the root of your angst. Are you in the wrong place with the wrong people in the wrong building? Or is everything around you wrong because you are living at a level below your potential?

The answers to these questions are telling. Take a moment and assess any frustration that is manifesting in your life. Instead of rearranging the deck chairs on your ship of life, get to the bottom of the issues you face. Commit to dealing with frustration head on so that you can evaluate your true capacity. Meanwhile, understand that frustration and other forms of suffering serve a purpose: they expand your capacity for greatness.

In Chapter 7, we talked about leveraging adversity Real people like Muhammad Ali fulfill their destinies when they learn how to leverage their suffering. They discover that they can expand their capacities by enduring trials and overcoming obstacles. It is one of the methods by which they become fit for the place of prominence.

You cannot rise to the level of destiny fulfillment without withstanding some opposition. Just as grueling political campaigns help candidates to rise to the demands of leadership, the tension between adversity and destiny fulfillment grooms *you* for high places. The capacity to take your territory and manage it successfully must be created. This is done largely through suffering.

To bear the burden of your destiny means (in part) to embrace and not curse your trials. Trials produce your capacity to handle life's blessings. This process is often lacking for those who become overnight sensations. The woeful stories of lottery winners who go bankrupt bears witness to the fact that, absent the created capacity for abundance and success, we invariably sabotage ourselves and our good fortune.

Suffering serves to increase capacity, but only if you deal with the pain. If you bury it, the pain will consume you. In the case of Joseph, the suffering of his brothers' betrayal enlarged his capacity for rulership. He leveraged his suffering during the worst of times. As a result, he found the strength to forgive and bless his brothers later in life. Not only that, but the formerly self-centered Daddy's boy developed true compassion for the plight of others.

Joseph's capacity was enlarged through his suffering. The tighter life's web seemed to wind around him, the bigger he became inside. Adversity revealed his emotional and spiritual muscle to break out, break through, and break into his destiny.

There comes such a time in every life. You may not be living in as a physical slave, but you will experience times of frustration and difficulty. That is when something in you must be stirred. The desire to grow—in the belief of your God-given destiny, in favor and prosperity, in influence for the greater good—must drive you to press through the tough membrane of your trial and into the open air of destiny fulfillment. Amazingly enough, the tighter the web that has been spun around you, the more your capacity can be expanded!

Suffering is not the only component of capacity enlargement. To increase your capacity for destiny fulfillment, you must also use what you have to its fullest measure. This includes your God-given abilities, resources, and experiences. Until you use them to their fullest measure, the next step of your journey will remain on hold. This dynamic is known as *The Law of Use.*

It is important to realize that The Law of Use must be implemented in the smallest of ways before it can be applied on a grand scale. We see this in the life of Muhammad Ali. When his bicycle was stolen, the sense of injustice stirred him to action. Ali responded by preparing himself to right the wrong. He had not set out to be a professional boxer; he started with a small dream—to punish a thief.

As the months and years wore on, however, Ali set his sights higher and higher. There came a time when beating up the Schwinn thief was no longer the goal—competing in the Olympics was! Having won the gold medal, Ali reset his sights on the world of professional boxing. Bout by bout, his capacity was enlarged. Little by little, he learned who he was and realized the extent of his professional prowess. It was a matter of time before he called himself and was recognized by others as "The Greatest."

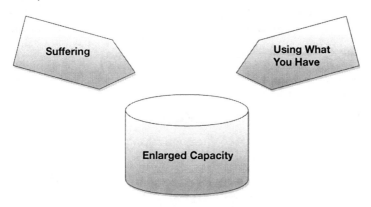

From Limitation to Enlargement

The expanding of your capacity is a form of growth. In the physical realm, growth requires certain conditions including, light, rest, sustenance, nurturing, and movement. In the realm of destiny fulfillment, the primary condition necessary for the growth of capacity is, ironically, the sense of limitation.

The sense of limitation is developed at a gut level and is a form of frustration. You cannot put your finger on it at first, but you feel constricted. It is as though you have outgrown your clothes; they served you well for a time, but now they restrict your movement and detract from your appearance. You can launder, iron, and accessorize them, but remain uncomfortable and unattractive.

In terms of destiny fulfillment, you feel constricted when you begin to sense that your destiny code is leading you to a "larger" place. Typically, it is a place where your gifts are used to a greater degree and are further developed. It is usually a place of increased influence; your gifts come to the attention of others, therefore you affect more people. In this larger place, priorities begin to shift in order to accommodate a larger, better-defined field of pursuit.

The place of limitation precedes the place of enlargement. You know that you have outgrown something and you are aware of the stifling effect of your cramped quarters. But you don't yet know how to get out of where you are or how to get where you are going. All you know is that you feel yourself being pulled into something bigger, something about which you are growing more curious each day.

This awareness of a new destination creates a hunger to leave what had previously been a comfortable place. Suddenly, all that seemed cozy begins to look old. The drapes are tired; the LaZboy creaks; the air is stale. Questions about what lies beyond the comfort zone no longer create anxiety. Instead, they feed curiosity churn your desire for the "next thing."

When you awaken to your feelings of constriction, you are ready to take the limits off your life. You understand that you are being pulled into something bigger because your surroundings look undersized, as though someone dropped you into a dollhouse-scale replica of your life. You sense the limitation because you see it in comparison with your destination. Your picture of that destination is necessarily incomplete, but your destiny code has engaged your imagination to the point where you know somewhere deep inside that you have bigger fish to fry.

Think It Through _____

Are you squirming in a constricted place? Do you feel yourself being pulled into something bigger? Is your destiny code speaking to you? What is it saying?

This is often when mentors show up. When Ali's bike was stolen, Joe Martin came alongside him. Martin helped Ali to get a clear picture of what his goal required of him. He helped Ali to create a framework within which his vision could be honed. Ali knew he wanted to fight the boy who harmed him. Martin knew Ali would have to prepare himself for the fight. This awakened in Ali the desire to do whatever was necessary to be ready.

Mentors awaken desire. When you feel the limitation, they model the place of enlargement. They provide a standard by which to judge your location and your progress. They confirm the place of limitation and point to the place into which your destiny code is pulling you. They affirm your desire for growth. When you point to the fence and swing your bat, your mentor will say, "Go for it, kid. That fence is yours to take."

Your mentor does not live under the cloud of your self-doubt or fear. Over the years, Muhammad Ali's various trainers (including Angelo Dundee) recognized his potential. They saw him wearing the champion's belt. During his fight with Sonny Liston, a caustic substance got into Ali's eyes. He began blinking furiously, in obvious pain. When he cried out saying that he could not see, his trainers did what they could to wash the substance out of his eyes.[13] But they addressed more than the physical problem; they addressed the emotional issues it had sparked:

> Dundee was frantic, trying to get his fighter back into the ring.
>
> "This is the big one," he pleaded, knowing that if Clay quit, the young fighter might never get another chance for the title. "You're fighting for the championship!"
>
> By the middle of the sixth round, the stinging in Clay's eyes had subsided.[14]

Your mentor will help you to think like an architect. He or she will train you to see the finished building before the foundation has been poured. Your mentor will help you to leave the place of limitation and enter the place of enlargement by holding the vision up before your hurting eyes. A good mentor will help you to see the end from the beginning, so to speak. When your vision is clouded over by adversity, your mentor will wash your eyes out and cheer you on.

Acknowledge Your Limitation

Are you in the place of limitation? Do you feel constricted? Do the things that once brought you glee now fail to satisfy? Are you ready to admit it? Are you willing to *say it* aloud?

If not, you misunderstand the feeling. Recognizing the place of limitation is not a sign of failure; it is a sign of growth. Until you come to this place and acknowledge it, your capacity cannot be enlarged. Do not misread the sense of constriction. It is not a place to avoided, but appreciated.

The place of limitation has great value, both for you and for those in whom you are willing to confide. Although you feel alone in the constricted place, you never are. There are always others who are grappling with the same feelings. They sense the constriction just as you do, but they are afraid to verbalize it just as you are. They may sit in the work cubicle next to yours or the pew behind yours at church. They are trying to keep up their image; they are holding up their façade. Just like you, they are trying to make other people think they have got their act together.

Everyone is afraid to confess feelings of constriction, at least at first. We don't want people to think we are unhappy. We feel too vulnerable to admit our dissatisfaction or to admit that we don't know how to get "there" from "here." Our fear reveals a lack of context for our feelings. We think that admitting the sense of limitation indicates that what we have or what we have achieved so far is not valuable. We fear that others will think we are dissatisfied with everything—our spouses, our kids, our homes, our professions.

But that is not what these feelings mean. What they really indicate is the knowledge that there is still more ahead. We are not satisfied to stop short of our ultimate destinations. We *need* to keep moving, growing, and raising the bar. It is our nature as natural-born destiny achievers.

It is also in our nature to reach plateaus. We see them as breaks in the battle; they are places in which we catch our breath and enjoy a sense of comfort. We were not created to stay there very long, however. We were designed to continue the upward climb at some point—the point at which the sense of limitation begins to stifle.

Transparency comes hard to most of us. Not only do we shrink from verbalizing the sense of limitation; we are also reticent to give voice to our dreams, desires, and destiny codes. Somewhere in the psyche, the self-editor warns that our dreams are too big or imaginary or grandiose. We become convinced that voicing them makes us look prideful or over-confident. So we choose what seems to be the safer path of self-deprecation, not realizing that false humility is an affectation. It is inauthentic and worse—it is pride dressed in a non-threatening disguise.

In a very real sense, we are afraid that if we pour out our hearts, no one will be there to listen or to pull us through into the place of enlargement. Quite the opposite is true. If we choose to be forthcoming, we make room for the very people who are positioned to help us.

Isolation and the Law of Reduction

If destiny fulfillment is your goal, be prepared to spend time in the "training room" of life. You won't have a lot of company there; just you and your dream. It is a spartan and often lonely incubator; but for those who dream of great exploits, the place of isolation is invaluable. For Muhammad Ali, the isolation investment was a prerequisite to greatness:

> Ali started his day off with early morning runs at 5:30 AM. He would stretch beforehand and then would run 6 miles a day in army type-boots in under 40 minutes. Ali made sure he ate a wholesome breakfast-all natural foods, oranje juice [sic], and plenty of water. After he ran, he would perform some exercises, stretching, and then go back home to get washed up. Ali then went to the gym at 12:30 PM for 3 hours

until 3:30 PM. After the gym, he would get a massage rub down, then get washed up. Then he would talk with the TV people, go out and enjoy himself, and then eat dinner. Ali said in his book, "I always ate good: chicken, steaks, green beans, potatoes, vegetables, fruit, juice and water." After dinner, he would go for a walk and relax by watching TV. Ali made sure he trained 6 days a week with one off day a week where he'd relax and ease his body and mind.[15]

It is easy to imagine that, while Ali subjected himself to this rigorous schedule, some of his friends opted for the carefree, off-the-cuff life young people naturally favor. They may have kidded Ali about all the fun they were having while he was training for his destiny. They may have joked about partying into the wee hours and going to bed at the same hour he awoke for his morning run. But Ali had a vision in mind. He was willing to delay his gratification so that he could accomplish something bigger than anything for which they were willing to contend.

When you submit to the place or season of isolation you are changed. You learn to distinguish between pursuits of promise and attractive, but unfruitful distractions. You realize that some of the things you thought were essential are not at all important. While they might facilitate comfort or a sense of security, you understand that they also dilute your vision and drain vital energy.

An honest pursuit of purpose will deliver you from distraction. With the precision of a surgeon, you cut the fat from your schedule. You skip the afternoon soap operas and invest in your own life story. You lose track of *American Idol,* but you live your own dream and attract those who are key to your unfolding destiny. Little by little, you drop the time-wasters and devote your hours to the things that are truly important—not to creating comfort zones, but to taking new, fertile territory.

When you become destiny-focused, something called the Law of Reduction kicks in. Anything that gets in the way of your development raises a red flag and screams, "Dead end!" Your destiny DNA guides your choices according to an inbred protocol that matches your activities to your stated goals. The leaner your schedule becomes, the more destiny rewards you reap. The hours you spend prospecting instead of vegetating add muscle to your client list. Your focused efforts draw the attention of others. Your willingness to articulate your dreams causes the right people to partner with you and add their firepower to yours.

The Law of Reduction simplifies your destiny path. Instead of looking hither and yon for solutions, comforts, and affirmation, your vision becomes laser-focused on the one thing—the essential thing you cannot live without.

What is the one thing a professional boxer cannot do without? Joe Martin showed Muhammad Ali what it was when he was just twelve years old: a well-trained, well-conditioned body. Ali continued to invest in his physical conditioning throughout his career. His schedule did not revolve around his personal wants and desires; it was built around his professional commitment. That is not to say that personal time is unimportant; it is critical to physical and mental health. The key is to have a plan that accommodates rest, recreation, and recovery time in a way that also advances the best use of your training time.

Ali trained hard six days a week and allowed for relaxation and recreation on the seventh day and every evening. He carved up his time wisely and enjoyed the long-term rewards of being "The Greatest."

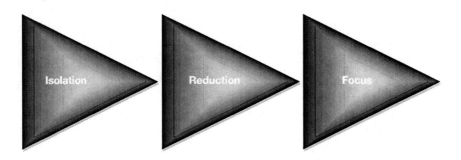

Isolation Develops Potential

For Muhammad Ali, the commitment to intense training separated him from others. That separation was a form of isolation. For Joseph, isolation was more literal: he was irrevocably separated from his family, his culture, and the everyday amenities of life. Joseph was alone in Egypt with nothing but his dream.

From his story, it is clear that Joseph cleaved to his dream. He suffered numerous injustices and was treated inhumanely. Yet, Joseph knew who he was. He recognized his destiny code and managed to rise to the top of the heap in every situation he faced.

Upon his arrival in Egypt, Joseph was sold to a prominent Egyptian named Potiphar, who was Pharaoh's captain of the guard.[16] Joseph served faithfully in Potiphar's home—so much so that Potiphar put Joseph in charge of his affairs and entrusted everything he owned to Joseph's care. With Joseph overseeing his household, Potiphar prospered. What an astounding accomplishment for a young slave!

Joseph was a strapping, handsome man. Potiphar's wife apparently found him irresistible. She made repeated advances, but was rebuffed by Joseph, who was loyal to Potiphar and refused to dishonor him. Nevertheless, Potiphar's wife continued to pursue Joseph. One day, when they were alone, she grabbed Joseph by his cloak and tried yet again to seduce him. Joseph fled, leaving his cloak behind.

Embittered at his rejection of her, Potiphar's wife accused Joseph of sexual assault. In defense of his wife's reputation, Potiphar had Joseph thrown into the dungeon. Betrayed once again, Joseph found himself in the lowest of low places. Yet, even there, Joseph's character and abilities were recognized. The prison warden put Joseph in charge of the entire prison operation! Everywhere he went, Joseph's destiny codes continued to motivate him to excel in every possible way.

The Law of Reduction operated in the extreme in Joseph's life. Having already been betrayed by his family, carried off to a foreign land, and now falsely accused and imprisoned, Joseph had been reduced to the irreducible minimum—a place of utter isolation in which he could see no conceivable hope of escape or improvement. Although Joseph was highly favored and given a great deal of responsibility, he would almost certainly live out his days in confinement.

Things had gone from bad to worse, yet Joseph persevered. No doubt, he had his share of bad days in which the weight of his situation felt crushing. The years of isolation were long and monotonous. But even the worst of circumstances could not snuff out his destiny codes. Instead, isolation brought Joseph to a place of clarity. Isolated and alone, Joseph learned what was really necessary: he reconnected with his unusual gift—his ability to interpret dreams.

Remember that the interpretation of dreams is what got Joseph into trouble in the first place. Interpreting his dreams for his brothers was the final straw in their rocky relationship. It landed him in Egypt, a place that seemed completely incongruous with his destiny. Yet, it was in Egypt that Joseph would realize what his unique factor was! It would come to light when two other unfortunate men found themselves thrown in prison after they displeased Pharaoh.

The Pharaoh's baker and cupbearer were assigned to Joseph's leadership. After being imprisoned for some time, each of the two men had a startling dream, with both dreams occurring on the same night. By now, Joseph knew them well enough to discern their moods and realized that the men were perturbed.

"Why are your faces so sad today?"[17] Joseph asked.

Then they said to him, "We have had a dream and there is no one to interpret it."[18]

Joseph immediately offered to interpret the men's dreams. For the cupbearer, the news was good: his dream foretold his release from prison and his restoration to his former position in Pharaoh's court. The baker was not as fortunate. His dream foretold his demise: within days Pharaoh would have him executed. Confident in the interpretations he provided, Joseph asked the cupbearer to remember him to Pharaoh in the hopes that he, too, might be released from prison. Sadly for the baker, both of Joseph's dream interpretations were accurate.

Having demonstrated his uncanny gift, Joseph hoped that the cupbearer would return the favor and promptly mention him to Pharaoh. Instead, the cupbearer forgot Joseph. For two years after the cupbearer's release, Joseph languished in prison alone. It looked as though his only hope for release had evaporated. We can only imagine the thoughts that plagued him: "How could the cupbearer forget me? Will it be another dozen years until my next opportunity comes along? Will I ever leave this place or will I rot in here and be forgotten forever?"

Joseph was a heavyweight in training. His days of isolation were painful but fruitful. His opportunity with the cupbearer was his Olympic gold medal. It helped to develop his potential and prepare him for what was ahead. He needed to train a little longer, add a little more bulk, and hang onto his dream.

Joseph's professional title bout was yet to come.

Download Your Code

1. Do you have a plan of self-development designed to prepare and propel you toward destiny fulfillment? What is your current "training regimen"?
2. In what areas of your life are you experiencing frustration? What is the source of the frustration and how can you use it to expand your capacity?
3. Are you using all the tools in your destiny "toolbox"? Are any of your gifts sitting on the shelf? Are you strengths being employed or set aside for "another day"? Explain.
4. What if any type of isolation are you currently experiencing? What benefit do you stand to gain? How close are you to your irreducible minimum? What does that foretell about your destiny achievement?
5. How is the place of isolation affecting your connection to your unique factor? How is your unique factor operating in the place of isolation?

Notes

1. Walter Dean Myers, *The Greatest: Muhammad Ali* (New York: Scholastic, 2001), 5-6.
2. Ibid., 6.
3. Ibid.
4. Ibid., 10, 12-13.
5. Muhammad Ali with Hana Yasmeen Ali, *The Soul of a Butterfly: Reflections on Life's Journey* (New York: Simon & Schuster, 2004), 10.
6. Ibid., 39.
7. Ibid., 15.
8. Ibid.
9. Myers, xiii.
10. "Muhammad Ali Boxing Workout," MuscleProdigy, http://www.muscleprodigy. com/muhammad-ali-boxing-workout-arcl-1051.html (accessed October 27, 2010).
11. Myers, xiv.

12. Ibid., xix.
13. Ibid., xviii.
14. Ibid.
15. "Muhammad Ali Boxing Workout."
16. The details of Joseph's story as noted in this chapter are taken from the Book of Genesis, chapters 37 and 39. All direct Bible quotes are documented individually.
17. Genesis 39:4-5.
17. Genesis 40:7 (New American Standard Bible).
18. Genesis 40:8 (New American Standard Bible).

9
Closing in on the Codes

...Most of the hardships we face provide us with opportunities to discover who we are meant to be and what we can share of our gifts to benefit others.

—Nick Vujicic, *Life Without Limits*

The name *Nick Vujicic* may or may not be familiar to you. If not, his quote about hardships might sound like a standard word of encouragement. When you understand the context from which he speaks, Vujicic's words take on added value:

> I am twenty-seven years old. I was born without any limbs, but I am not constrained by my circumstances. I travel the world encouraging millions of people to overcome adversity with faith, hope, love, and courage so that they may pursue their dreams.[1]

Nick Vujicic is an overcomer. He speaks to adversity with the authority of one who has experienced its full fury. Having endured uncommon tribulation, Vujicic has come through it with unquenchable joy and a clear sense of his destiny code. Today, he is a minister and public speaker who impacts lives around the world. Vujicic has accomplished all of this despite and even because of the difficulties he has faced

Vujicic's story is raw and remarkable. He entered the world, not as the celebrated firstborn, but as one met with gasps of sorrow and unending tears. Vujicic's early years were tough; he suffered many emotional blows throughout his youth. Much of his earliest history was locked in the vault of infant memory; but Vujicic probed his parents and bravely sought the truth about his first days. Their tender but frank accounts filled in the blanks for Vujicic, but created, at least at first, fresh wounds that would need to be healed.

Although Nick and his family have experienced the glories of redemption for all of their suffering, the facts of Nick's birth reveal remind us of the rough terrain the Vujicics crossed in those early years:

> My parents are devout Christians, but after I was born with neither arms nor legs, they wondered what God had in mind in creating me. At first, they assumed that there was no hope and no future for someone like me, that I would never live a normal or productive life.[2]

Nick's parents were completely unprepared for his condition. Ultrasounds had revealed no abnormalities or concerns.[3] Nick's mother had worked as a midwife and pediatric nurse. She knew the prenatal drill and followed all the recommended protocols to ensure the health of her baby.[4] But in the delivery room, it was clear that something was wrong. When Mrs. Vujicic asked whether her baby was all right, no one responded—and no one put little Nick in her arms, at least not at first.[5]

Mrs. Vujicic's professional experience left no doubt; something was terribly wrong, but what? She began to panic. Soon, the doctors answered her queries; they pronounced her son's condition in clinical terms indicating the absence or malformation of limbs.[6] Shock and denial set in. Mrs. Vujicic had yet to learn the full extent of her son's disability.

Outside the delivery room, Vujicic's father was informed of his son's condition. No details were withheld. Grief-stricken, but concerned for his wife, he hoped to break the news gently. But it was too late. Mrs. Vujicic's protective wall of shock and denial had been pierced through in a crushing instant[7] as the delivery team covered Nick and brought him to her.

Her anguish was overwhelming. Shaken to her core and unable to confront the visible evidence of the difficult news, she said, "Take him away. I don't want to touch him or see him."[8]

Think It Through _____

Have you ever been so shocked by events that you behaved in ways you never imagined you would? What helped you to move past the shock and into the processing of your pain?

Patterns: Rejection and Betrayal

Nick's parents did what most of us do at some point in life: they questioned everything, including God.[9] The enormity of their emotional and spiritual battle is understandable, especially since they had no warning of Nick's condition. It is hard to imagine how they would *not* have felt betrayed.

Although their faith ultimately led the Vujicic family through the quagmire of emotions and heartbreak, the truth of their initial trauma is an important part of their story. They experienced a significant emotional event involving the most significant people in their lives—each other. Such events are not just about the present; they are about the future. They are among the symbols and signals that comprise our destiny codes.

Nick Vujicic had many battles to wage for himself. Growing up is hard for everyone. For a youth with no limbs and one oddly placed foot, the difficulties increase exponentially. Some children accepted Vujicic, but others called him cutting names like "freak and alien."[10] Like every other child, Vujicic longed for acceptance. He tried to blend in with the crowd, but to no avail. He felt alone, worried about the future, and hopeless.[11]

Nick's preteen years were particularly challenging:

> ...I won [my classmates] over with my wit, my willingness to poke fun at myself, and by throwing my body around on the playground. On my worst days I hid behind the shrubbery or in empty classrooms to avoid being hurt or mocked.[12]

Perhaps the most painful rejection came when Nick pressed his parents to tell him about his birth. They were careful to wait until Nick had gained sufficient emotional strength and maturity to deal with their honesty. They did not give him a sugar-coated tale, but the true story of their early struggles. They even shared Mrs. Vujicic's order in the delivery room to take her baby out of her sight.

> ...when my mum told me that she didn't want to hold me after I was born, it was hard to take, to say the least. I was insecure enough as it was, but to hear that my own mother could not bear to look at me was...well, imagine how you might feel. I was hurt and I felt rejected...[13]

Remember: significant emotional events are always about the future. They create a platform for your future by developing your gifts, abilities, and character. The profound rejection Nick Vujicic experienced strengthened his character and empowered him to persevere. The challenges demanded of him a level of tenacity and creativity that enabled him not only to survive, but to develop a level of independence and self-sufficiency.

Rejection and other patterns of suffering equipped Vujicic for his future ministry. His experiences produced an authenticity compassion rarely produced in the absence of pain. When he speaks to individuals or crowds or shares his surfing adventures, he touches a nerve that few people even know exists. Nick Vujicic is uniquely qualified to address the fears and emotional wounds of others. He is gifted to encourage them to live ridiculously happy lives.

By facing his pain and moving on, Vujicic tapped into and cooperated with his destiny code. He found value in significant emotional events. He had the courage to demand the truth and overcome the pain it caused. He confronted the downside of his circumstances and placed the negatives inside the context of his life's bigger picture. With this broader perspective in place, Vujicic was free to advance from season to season and opportunity to opportunity.

Unless we tackle the obvious issues we face, we will spend our lifetimes enduring endless cycles of setback. Situations will arise that look and sound different, but will be born of the same old dynamic of defeat. This is the way the symbols and signals of our destiny codes work. They demand to be understood. When they are, forward motion is the natural result, even when great difficulties challenge our progress.

Consider the rejection that marked Nick Vujicic's life. Had he not confronted the terrible pain of it, he would have carried the resulting defense mechanisms into every activity, relationship, and opportunity that came along. Every future situation would have been interpreted through the lens of fear that caused him to hide behind the bushes as a child. Intimidation, memories of humiliation, and risk aversion would have hemmed him in and imposed a lifestyle of stagnancy.

Would Vujicic have considered getting on a surfboard or speaking before large audiences in that state of mind? Probably not. If you feared being cruelly mocked for the thousandth time, would you get on a surfboard with no arms or legs? Would you stand before staring crowds of people as Vujicic does? Can you see how important it is to process the patterns of your suffering?

Unless we understand that seasons of rejection are part of life, we will forever bemoan life's imperfections and wait for conditions to be perfect before moving forward. Until we come to grips with rejection and develop the strength of character to risk being rejected again, we will never take the risky steps that lead to destiny fulfillment. Just as we must embrace seasons of isolation, we must accept and understand the meaning of our seasons of rejection.

Both help us to discover our true identities and unlock our destiny codes. Often, the two are closely connected.

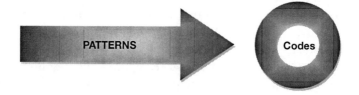

Embrace Your Personal History

Each of us has learned multitudes of lessons in life. Often, the most powerful ones are learned through adversity, when we are the most desperate for answers and the most open to truth. All forms of suffering, including feelings of limitation, isolation, rejection, disappointment, and loss can lead us to the truth we seek, but only if we learn to accept suffering and other life experiences as meaningful parts of our personal history.

Personal history is more than the documentation of life's low points. Personal history is the sum total of your life. It is comprised of four basic elements:

1. *The environment.* This is the life context in which you are shaped. Some elements of your environment include your family setting, culture, religious beliefs, and neighborhood influences. These factors impact the formation of your overall belief system and, therefore, your behavior. Elements of your environment, whether positive or negative, can serve to hold you back or release you into the unfolding of your destiny code. It all depends upon how you respond.

2. *Heredity.* This is your physical DNA; it can affect physical and mental health, areas of gifting, and your appearance. All of these factors play into the unfolding of your life story. For example, the formative experiences of a chronically ill child are different from those of a healthy child. It is important to note that the effect of DNA on outcomes varies according to your response to the challenges you face. Not everyone who is born with Nick Vujicic's physical impairments will flourish to the degree Vujicic has. In his case, poor outcomes were mitigated by a positive, hopeful approach to adversity.

3. *Identity.* This is your intuitive knowledge of self. It is the deep down recognition of your place as a unique human being. It involves the understanding of your inherent worth apart from externals such as what you do and how you look. Authentic identity is at the very core of your being. It is not based on performance, although your sense of identity affects your performance. Your identity is based upon who you were created to be.

4. *Total life experience.* Everything you have said, done, heard, seen, tasted, felt, dreamed, believed, and experienced up to this moment is part of your total life experience. Your environment, heredity, and identity are part of your total life experience, too. All four elements comprise the complete story of your life: *your personal history.*

YOUR PERSONAL HISTORY

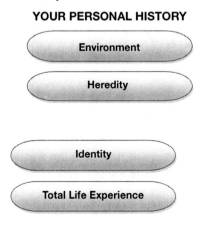

When you embrace your personal history, you accurately assess the value of every element of your life. You extract meaning from all of it. You realize that, in the course of living, you have accrued valuable resources that can be applied as a down payment on your destiny fulfillment.

Some of your resources are tangible: you may have an advanced degree in biochemistry that opens doors in your field. Other resources are intangible, such as your ability to think creatively. Both equip you to make measurable progress on your destiny path. Your resume grows; you form key relationships; you develop a reputation in the industry.

Both separately and combined with other things you have learned and become, these resources have great value. They are a form of equity resulting from your personal history. Even the parts of your personal history that you would rather forget add value to your destiny pursuit. You thought they made you a loser or a failure, but they prepared you for success. Don't waste these unattractive pieces—they are part of your equity.

How can we achieve great things unless we are prepared to bear the burden and finish the course? Nick Vujicic had a tough time of life, but he built up a ton of equity. That equity is paying off in the form of destiny fulfillment:

> All events come together for the good. I'm certain of that because it's been true in my life. What good is a life without limbs? Just by looking at me, people know that I faced and overcame many obstacles and hardships. That makes them willing to listen to me as a source of inspiration. They allow me to share my faith, to tell them they are loved, and to give them hope. That is my contribution.[14]

It is often in the act of overcoming difficulty that we develop a heightened awareness of our identities. The very experiences and characteristics you thought counted you out are often the things in your life that are most precious—and powerful.

> You may hit hard times. You may fall down and feel as though you don't have the strength to get back up. I know the feeling, mate. We all do. Life isn't always easy, but when we overcome challenges, we become stronger and more grateful for our opportunities. What really matters are the lives you touch along the way and how you finish your journey.[15]
>
> —Nick Vujicic

Back to Your Future

There is another key to accurately understanding your personal history. When you understand this key, you will find meaning and value in all of your life. Ready? Here it is: *Your responses to your present affect your future, but your future also determines your present.*

Let's take some time to digest this important concept. You already know that the decisions you make today leave their mark on tomorrow. But that is only half of the story. Your tomorrow—your destiny—is the reason certain things happen today.

Mind-boggling, isn't it? Nevertheless, if you look back over your life you will see specific evidences that it is true. Did you meet your future mate because you missed your usual morning train? Did you sell your clothing line to Marshall Field because you "bumped into" someone, as Cynthia Rowley did?

Nothing about your life is accidental. You are a human being, a superior being as compared say, to members of the animal kingdom. You are completely unique; therefore, your personal history is unique and uniquely designed by your Creator to produce the fulfillment of your purpose—your *destiny*. Your gifts exist to complement your purpose; significant emotional events (which involve significant people in your life) prepare you for your purpose; your passions motivate the pursuit of purpose.

Nick Vujicic's childhood struggles were part and parcel of a beautiful design that pointed to the future he is living today. Did he see all of that when he hid behind the shrubbery in the schoolyard? Probably not. But even as he shuddered in fear and intimidation, he was discovering his destiny codes. He was learning about whom he was and whom he was created to be. He found out that he was stronger than he thought. He tapped into the desire to help others. As his personal history played out, his future story was revealed.

Because we are human and because the maturation of our destiny codes is a process, we do not always see how the future drives our current experiences. The more aware we become of our destiny codes, however, the more astute this recognition will be.

To Recycle or Not to Recycle

One of the keys of making your personal history work for you is to know which parts to recycle and which to release. Have you ever held onto something—an attachment from an old vacuum or the feed tube from an obsolete juicer—only to have it clutter your closet and gather dust?

Recycling is not about stashing stuff. It is about putting it to future use. Often, we recycle our emotional trash, not by re-purposing it, but by rehearsing it. Instead of learning from painful experiences and moving on, we dredge them up again and again and superimpose them on our future experiences.

If you have been married more than once, you probably understand this dynamic. Let's assume that your first husband was unfaithful. You remember the pain of his dalliances; they were significant emotional events. Instead of processing the pain and using it as preparation for your future; you drag it in all its unprocessed awfulness into your new marriage.

Let's assume that you are now married to a man who loves you and honors your relationship. He works hard to avoid temptation altogether. Because your pain is unprocessed, the same old fears remain attached to it. You live in constant dread of being abandoned for another woman.

One day, your husband runs to the store for a quart of milk and is gone forty minutes instead of ten. All the old alarms begin sounding in your head.

"Oh no, it's happening again," you fret. "He is probably flirting with some 'dish' in the supermarket. I can't believe this is happening to me after all I've been through."

When your husband walks in the door, your Code-Red frame of mind has obliterated your ability to reason. Instead of saying, "Thanks, honey. I appreciate your going out in this awful rain," you ask questions that reveal your distrust.

Before he can explain that he helped an elderly man change a flat tire…before you notice his blackened hands and soiled parka, you bring the failure or your previous marriage between the two of you. By the time the facts are known, emotional wounds from the past have bred new ones in the present.

You have succumbed to a state of existence in which you keep recycling old, rotten trash. Because of unresolved pain, the most unattractive elements of your personal history have become permanent reference points. You keep dragging out the old trash and the more you do it, the more trapped you feel. You expect the old cycles and patterns to reemerge, even though your current circumstances do not support your conclusion. Without realizing it, you have reinforced obsolete, outdated limits on your life. You have assigned yourself to a return engagement on the trash pile.

There is a good kind of recycling of your personal history. This one doesn't just rehash the old trash; instead, it promotes renewal. Healthy recycling allows for a reset and adaptation. In the case of the remarried couple, the wife would have realized that she was being emotionally triggered by old trash. Having made that determination, she would have been free to discard the template of her previous relationship (reset) and bring a clean slate to her new one. Instead of reacting in fear-based ways, she would respond (adapt) on the basis of new information.

Don't misunderstand me; it *is* easy to fall into the recycle bin of old hurts. However, you can choose to take a fresh look at new situations. They do not have to be viewed and evaluated strictly according to past experiences.

Nick Vujicic has recycled the painful experiences of his formative years and chosen to share them with others. He is not drudging up the past for the sake of rehearsal; he is recycling the valuable experiences he has processed and repurposed. As a result, he brings hope to those who are discouraged and even heartbroken.

Good recycling is about recovery. When you recycle plastics, they don't pile up in a landfill leeching toxins and clogging the environment. Instead, their intrinsic value is recovered and applied to a new use. When you properly recycle your personal history, you recover its value and apply it purposefully to the betterment of your future and to the benefit of others.

Instead of creating a toxic, cluttered landfill, you foster personal renewal and productivity.

RECOVER   **RESET**

ADAPT

RECYCLE AS RENEWAL

Refuse to Be Trapped in Your Past

When you recycle the material of your personal history in productive ways, you use all of it, including patterns of suffering, to your advantage.

In Chapter 2, we talked about accepting the past. Francisco Bucio accepted the fact that his right hand, his primary surgical tool, had been crushed under tons of rubble during an earthquake. Once he understood that he could not change what happened to him, he was able to move forward in productive ways and arrive at a useful new approach to his future. He recycled his expectations and embraced a series of unconventional surgical procedures that would restore the use of his hand, albeit not the way he imagined.

At some level, he recognized that his destiny code was contained within the events that almost crushed his dream of being a plastic surgeon. He cooperated with his code and made the decisions that led to the preservation of his dream and a lucrative future.

Nick Vujicic never had a fully functional body. He had to deal with reality and decide whether he would succumb to disability or discover his destiny. He refused to be trapped in the past. The facts of his birth were not enough to convince him to live an unproductive life. Instead, he turned the tables on his disability and found within it a powerful purpose.

It is impossible to calculate the impact of Vujicic's refusal to be a victim. Already, hundreds of thousands have viewed his videos. His story is the kind people share with friends. How many lives have been touched is impossible to say. This much is certain: the impact of one well-lived life is *exponential.*

Four Phases of Your Dream

You have seen your destiny code from many angles over the course of this book. Let's take a quick tour of the workings of the dream your destiny code supports.

Like everything else in life, your dream has a process that continues from beginning to fulfillment. Your dream never leaves you, even when you ignore or shelve it. Its progress, however, can be hindered by your failure to acknowledge or engage it. But once you plug into your dream it will move through stages of development that keep *it* viable and *you* motivated.

What is your dream? Here is a brief primer on the subject from my book, *Live Your Dream*:

> Consider your life's dream a snapshot of the future that awaits your arrival.... Using your "snapshot" as your standard, you can evaluate your progress every step of the way and make adjustments designed to correct your course and manage shifting tides. *Your dream is a powerful image of your desired outcomes; it enables you to see the finish line from the starting gate.*[16]

The starting gate of your dream is what Robert Clinton from Fuller University calls *foundational processing.*[17] This part of the learning process about your dream and destiny is foundational to your cooperation. It is a time of discovery, not designed to give you goose bumps (although it might), but to propel you into the new levels of understanding and accountability that are requisite for destiny fulfillment. It is the place where you realize that significant turns of events hinge on small decisions. This is where you begin to see the interconnectedness of your choices, actions, relationships, and outcomes. You become sensitive enough to perceive the information that used to slip under your radar.

Foundational processing is where you get your destiny legs. For Nick Vujicic, this may have been the stage at which he began asking his parents very serious and difficult questions about the day of his birth. He needed to know the facts so that he could come to his own conclusions about his life and purpose. There is a point in life when each of us becomes sufficiently tuned in to the bigger picture to realize that, until we see our experiences within a larger context, we cannot find our assignments.

The second phase of your dream is *transition.* Often this is the point at which you realize you are headed some place you never dreamed of. Joseph entered transition when he was kidnapped and carried off to Egypt. It was an event of monumental proportions, in part because he never saw it coming. Until that day, Joseph fully expected to live and develop within the context of family.

The transition phase of your dream is where you switch gears and enter a growth period that prepares you for destiny fulfillment. Your growth period won't always look like growth. Often, it looks like giant leaps backward. Yet, even this incongruity serves to uncover and develop your natural abilities, intuition, and wisdom in decision-making.

Your growth period is the season during which the practical threads of your destiny code surface and begin moving in unison. This is where Joseph's leadership and dream interpretation skills were honed and put to practical use. Although he probably felt stuck in his situation, Joseph was being groomed for something much bigger than he could have imagined.

The final phase of your dream is *maturity*. Not only do the threads of your destiny code begin to flow in a particular direction, but everything starts fitting together. It is the "aha" moment when you say, "Now I understand why I am here. I see now what I was built for. This is my moment. I've been preparing for it all my life. Everything that happened brought me here for *this* purpose."

What a moment that is! It is the destiny threshold in which your effectiveness ramps up, your capabilities find the ideal environment in which to flourish, and you realize that the greatest pain in life is not all the mess you have been through—it is the pain of having potential and never reaching it.

For Joseph, the maturity phase was the point at which the dreams that seemed to languish for thirteen years came to life in a moment of time.

PHASES OF YOUR DREAM
1. FOUNDATIONAL PROCESSING
2. TRANSITION
3. GROWTH
4. MATURITY

Relationships: Your Destiny Context

Your destiny can never be fulfilled in the absence of relationships. As you have seen already, and will see more clearly in the next chapter, other people are positioned to catapult you into the fulfillment of your destiny code. These people play significant roles in your life and will be part of the significant emotional events you experience. They may be mentors, friends, family members, and even enemies.

Let's be frank: we all know people we don't like. Sometimes our dislike is based on other people's treatment of us. Sometimes, we blame bad "chemistry." Whatever the source of contention, our not-so-favorite people play as large a role in the Creator's grand design of destiny fulfillment as those who are supportive and loving. Like Joseph's cruel brothers, they serve to launch us into the places we really need to be.

Whether by their rejection or because of the isolation they prompt, our enemies prod us to grow. They help us to unlock our destiny codes and often our leadership potential. These folks cause us to look inward and help us to narrow down our interpretations of past events.

Whether pleasant or not, relationships create the context within which destiny unfolds. When you recognize the context, you realize that you have been inserted into a matrix of people and relationships that promote forward motion—for you *and* for those in your life. Within this matrix, you discover the power of networking and the exponential availability of resources networking makes possible.

Often, the providential connections that unlock your potential and your kernel of power are discovered when you are in the lost place and realize that you can't get out on your own. Found people don't ask for directions; lost people do. In the lost place you become more open to interacting with unlikely people—those from different backgrounds and experiences, those who see the world differently from you. They are the very ones you might have ignored before you were lost. Now, you see their value and recognize their role in your life.

It is important to understand the counterintuitive aspect of providential connections. Why? Because we typically want *certain* people or *certain kinds* of people to come alongside us. We see them as being compatible or gifted in a way that we think fits our dreams.

Have you ever been disappointed to find that the people you hoped for were not available or on board when you needed them? Could that be a clue? I believe it is. Sometimes the people you think you need will do more harm than good. If you assume for the wrong reasons that they are the right people, they will get in the way of your finding the truly providential connections that will best serve you.

These are the ones with whom you "magically" intersect at pivotal points on your destiny path. They are the ones who know how to pull you into the new place; they are the ones who become, or lead you to, pipelines of supply you never knew existed.

These previously invisible lines of supply are critical to your destiny fulfillment. If you knew the full extent of your potential, you would realize that you could never finance it on your own. But when you network, you interconnect with chains of supply that are greater than any you could summon alone.

Yes. Your dream *is* that big. You are going to need more resources than you think! Not only that but somebody, somewhere is going to follow you to the very place you are going.

This is not just about your destiny. It is about blazing a trail for others!

Download Your Code

1. How have patterns of rejection, betrayal, or other forms of suffering served to daunt you in the past? What valuable information might they reveal about your destiny?
2. Before beginning this book, how would you have characterized your personal history? How might you reinterpret it now? What can you learn from specific high points and perceived low points in your personal history?
3. Have you discovered ways in which you have recycled life's "trash" in the past? Describe any toxic effects. How might you improve your recycling skills and thereby promote renewal?
4. Understanding that the four cycles of your dream are not always perfectly linear and sometimes overlap, which cycle of your dream is most prominent in your life at this time? Which factors lead you to this conclusion?
5. Are/were there any relationships in your life that you now realize are/were providentially designed to promote your destiny fulfillment? What about these relationships led you to misidentify them?

Notes

1. Nick Vujicic, *Life Without Limits: Inspiration for a* Ridiculously *Good Life,* (New York: Doubleday, 2010) *vii.*
2. Ibid.
3. Ibid., 4.
4. Ibid., 3.
5. Ibid., 4.
6. Ibid.
7. Ibid., 4-5.
8. Ibid., 5.
9. Ibid.
10. Ibid., viii.

11. Ibid.

12. Ibid., 17.

13. Ibid., 6.

14. Ibid., 3.

15. Ibid., x.

16. Dr. Mark J. Chironna, *Live Your Dream,* (Shippensburg, PA: Destiny Image Publishers, 2009), 18-19.

17.

10
Your Macro Moment

Small opportunities are often the beginning of great enterprises.

—Demosthenes

His life had the drama of a Shakespearean tragedy. It was loaded with significant emotional events, lost seasons, periods of constriction and isolation, and significant others who blessed or cursed him. He'd seen a series of highs and lows: the highs were notable; the lows were abysmal. He had a knack for mastery; in the worst of circumstances, he always found a way to build something of value—a smooth operation, wealth for his employers, enhanced skills, service to others.[1]

His excellence was noticed. There was always someone who wanted to put him in charge of something. Even as an outsider and cultural alien, he was enormously trusted, given free reign over a large operation and even over a personal fortune. Everything he touched turned to gold in someone else's bank account.

Imprisoned and living behind the slammed door of injustice, his sentence had no end date. He continued to do good deeds that benefited others, although none of them was inclined or empowered to set him free. He looked to be forsaken—a gifted man with big dreams but no place to live out their fullness.

That is, until his macro moment came and everything would change.

Your Defining Moment

Two years earlier, Joseph asked Pharaoh's cupbearer to mention him to Pharaoh. You remember what happened: Joseph had interpreted the cupbearer's dream foretelling the man's release from prison and return to Pharaoh's good graces. When the man's dream came true, he forgot all about Joseph.

Now, two years later, Pharaoh was deeply troubled by dreams of his own. He called in his magicians and seers and asked them to interpret his dreams, but none succeeded. Suddenly, the cupbearer remembered the man in prison who interpreted dreams flawlessly. He mentioned the man to Pharaoh.

Joseph did not know it yet, but his defining moment had arrived. Its roots had been planted long ago, but the shoot just broke ground. The dream that had been incubating in Joseph's heart since his youth was about to be fulfilled. All the little decisions made during his lifetime had led him to this moment. All of his suffering and overcoming had created within him a sharpened awareness. It was the very thing that made him sensitive to the sad faces of the baker and cup-bearer on the day after their alarming dreams. Compassion drove him to help them; it may have seemed a simple decision at the time, but it was crucial. Now, it was about to pay off with a benefit that would affect millions.

Joseph's full potential was being unlocked. He had been a heavyweight in training for years. Now he was ready to step into the ring and take the title. It was opportunity on a grand scale, a chance for Joseph to meet his destiny by becoming Pharaoh's solution—not only to the problem of his dreams, but to a larger crisis he did not yet know about! Pharaoh recognized his need and summoned Joseph to the grand stage of his court.

Imagine Joseph's reaction as he shaved and changed his clothes! Imagine the thoughts racing through his mind as he was ushered from the dungeon into the opulence of Pharaoh's world! Joseph's thoughts are not recorded, but we know from his performance before Pharaoh that the man who flourished under the worst of circumstances, was also a man prepared to make the most of his moment.

"Pharaoh said to Joseph, 'I have had a dream, but no one can interpret it; and I have heard it said about you, that when you hear a dream you can interpret it.'"[2]

Since his experience with the cupbearer and baker Joseph had come to understand his unique factor well. He also understood the origin of his gift. After giving God credit, Joseph assured Pharaoh that God would enable Joseph to convey the meaning of the two dreams Pharaoh was about to describe. When Pharaoh was finished, Joseph explained what they meant: Egypt and the region would have seven years of plenty followed by seven years of drought.

The implications were enormous. Drought could destroy a nation as reliant on agriculture as Egypt was. The resulting famine could kill multitudes and jeopardize Pharaoh's wealth.

Think It Through _____

Identify a defining moment in your life. Describe the emotions you experienced. How did you respond? How was your life's momentum affected? What effects remain?

The Law of the Missing Piece

Joseph understood the ramifications of his defining moment. He knew that, if he mastered it, he would meet the need of the most powerful man on earth. If he failed, his life could take a turn for the worse. Remember: Joseph lived for at least two years hoping to make contact with Pharaoh. He told the cupbearer to mention his name to the ruler. Now, Joseph had his chance. He knew that this moment could launch him into all he was called to be, do, and have. He also knew that the moment was powerful because of Pharaoh. Pharaoh held what Joseph needed: his *missing piece.*

Because relationships are the context in which destiny unfolds, somebody else holds your missing piece. Yes. There is a person who holds the piece you are searching for. They await your arrival! This is not a one-sided transaction. You bring something to the table, too. In the providential order of things, you hold the other party's missing piece. Pharaoh was positioned to change Joseph's life, but Joseph was prepared to help Pharaoh avert disaster.

Unless you understand the importance of your missing piece, you cannot cooperate with your destiny code. You will miss your moment and fail to reach the position of influence you were created to fill. Had Joseph not understood this, he might have appeared before Pharaoh unshaven, improperly dressed, and disoriented. (After thirteen years in a filthy dehumanizing prison, this could easily have happened.)

Pharaoh might well have taken one look at Joseph and sent him away before he uttered a word. Or Joseph might have caved under the pressure of the moment and surrendered to self-doubt. He was, after all, standing before the most powerful and presumably most intimidating man in the world. Joseph might have cowered and excused himself, afraid to risk making a mistake before a man known for removing the heads of his closest aides.

But Joseph understood the transaction perfectly. He'd read his destiny codes. He knew Pharaoh had his missing piece. And he knew he had Pharaoh's. This was Joseph's moment and he seized it.

What exactly do I mean by *the missing piece?* It is the piece that causes the remaining pieces of your destiny puzzle to come alive. It might be a piece of information that helps you to complete a revolutionary mathematical formula. It could be an invitation to demonstrate your new product for Walmart buyers. Your missing piece could be an opportunity to fill in for a fabled musician and strut your musical stuff during a recording session attended by industry heavyweights.

Everybody's missing piece looks different; but everybody's missing piece has the same effect: it thrusts you into *the* place you need to be. It is someplace you could not conjure on your own. It exposes you to resources you could not muster by yourself. It brings input and exposure you could not buy for any amount of money.

Until his macro moment arrived, Joseph didn't have all the pieces of his destiny puzzle. He was skilled, highly regarded, smart, wise, and gifted. He knew he had a big destiny, but the picture was incomplete. *Something* was missing. Joseph had lots of pieces arranged in his mind, but until he had them all, he would remain in a stall pattern.

What Joseph needed was Pharaoh, the man who could change the dynamics of his life. The missing elements Joseph needed for the fulfillment of his destiny were Pharaoh's to give. And now, Pharaoh needed Joseph.

Bingo!

But why did it take so long for Joseph to find his missing piece? Joseph had begun interpreting dreams years earlier. Couldn't he have been called upon sooner? His destiny code had been working throughout his lifetime. So had Pharaoh's. So why did Joseph have to jump through hoop after awful hoop before reaching his macro moment?

Think about Joseph's personal history: we know he was phenomenally gifted at dream interpretation. We also know that his gift was working by the time he was seventeen years old. That is when Joseph correctly interpreted two of his own dreams. But think of how he bungled his delivery. He was brash, insensitive, and self-centered. He never stopped to consider the effect of his dreams on his already agitated brothers. Instead, Joseph was so excited about what his dreams meant for his own life that he forget to think about how his brothers would feel. Instead of creating a beautiful family moment, Joseph threw a lighted match onto an emotional powder keg.

Joseph was not yet prepared to handle his gift. You might not be prepared when you first receive *your* dream, either. It is always bigger than you—much bigger than you can imagine. It takes time to grow into it. You have to learn, often through periods of isolation, frustration, and rejection how to handle your dream and the people it affects.

When your dream first becomes evident, you think you know what you want, but you don't, at least not entirely. For one thing, you have not yet assessed all your dream will cost. You do not yet recognize how powerfully you can impact and even hurt others with your dream. Only after you process your dream and *it processes you* can you be ready to step into all that it demands.

Joseph the teenager was not ready to stand before Pharaoh, for several reasons. He might not have appreciated the importance of the encounter. Instead of finding his missing piece, Joseph might have lost his head, as the baker did. His immaturity and lack of understanding might have infuriated rather than helped Pharaoh. Not only that, but the day that Joseph was called up was the *right* day: it was the precise moment at which both men recognized their mutual need. Each knew that the other held his missing piece. The situation was perfectly ripe and would benefit everyone involved.

Joseph recognized the moment. It was the very thing for which he had hungered for years. He'd knocked on lots of doors during his journey: he served Potiphar well; he served the prison warden faithfully and met the needs of the inmates; he did right by the cupbearer. Yet his knocking did not seem to get him anywhere—until now. In reality, all of it was important. Every step, even the botched ones, had led him here. But now, all of it had come together. The deal was ready to be sealed and Joseph was ready for the transaction.

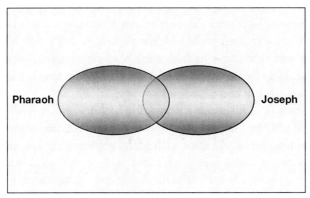

The Mutuality of the Missing Piece

Beggars Need Not Apply

Joseph delivered the interpretations of Pharaoh's dreams. Without waiting for Pharaoh to respond and without so much as an invitation to continue, Joseph initiated the next step on his destiny path. He boldly offered Pharaoh a solution to the coming drought, saying:

> And now let Pharaoh look for a discerning and wise man and put him in charge of the land of Egypt. Let Pharaoh appoint commissioners over the land to take a fifth of the harvest of Egypt during the seven years of abundance. They should collect all the food of these good years that are coming and store up the grain under the authority of Pharaoh, to be kept in the cities for food. This food should be held in reserve for the country, to be used during the seven years of famine that will come upon Egypt, so that the country may not be ruined by the famine.[3]

Joseph's unique factor was his entry ticket through the open door of opportunity. Now, he drew upon his well-honed administrative and communication skills to help Pharaoh realize how much he needed Joseph's expertise. His boldness paid off. Pharaoh recognized *his* missing piece. Joseph received the ultimate promotion. Pharaoh put him in charge of an entire nation!

Notice Joseph's mindset. Even though he had lived in obscurity for thirteen years, he did not grovel. He not only answered the ruler's questions; he also stated his opinions and cleverly created for himself a top position in Egypt's government.

Joseph had not come before Pharaoh as a beggar. He knew his destiny code. He was not ashamed to knock on this door of opportunity with the authority of someone who knew he belonged there. He was not afraid to draw attention to himself—not as a boaster, but as a problem solver. Joseph knew he had been groomed his whole life for something big and he knew this was it.

Joseph might not have been this sure of himself during his first eleven years in Egypt. But when he crossed paths with the cupbearer and the baker, he realized who he really was. He knew he had something significant—something other people needed. His circumstances would not change for another two years, but his mindset had already been transformed.

Now, Joseph was in his destiny prime. He had developed gradually through every season of his life. He paid attention to the symbols and signals of his destiny code. Even in the humblest of settings, he grew as a person and as a leader. He learned to steward what was not his and to do it with excellence. As a slave he learned to persevere. He held onto his dream, even when destiny achievement seemed impossible.

Joseph did not come before Pharaoh as a battered, beggarly, weary, disgruntled victim. He stood before Pharaoh as man with a plan; a willing participant in a transaction between two men destined for greatness.

The Crosswalk of Convergence

If you are tuned into your destiny code, your skills and abilities will become so refined as to come together in a defining moment that typically produces your missing piece. This is what happened to Joseph.

Joseph assessed his defining moment accurately. It was clear to him that Pharaoh lacked the understanding of what his dreams meant. Without this knowledge, Pharaoh could not address the warning his dreams provided. He had everything to lose. Without access to Joseph's multiple gifts, Egypt would have been at the mercy of the elements.

The slave standing before Pharaoh had found his niche. You can imagine the synapses firing in Joseph's brain. No doubt, he saw the dreams that had gotten him into trouble with his brothers and now saw the perfect sense they made. All of his bitter experiences began adding up to something wonderful. After years of suffering because of it, Joseph's uniqueness was revealed as the treasure it had always been. And truly, the best was yet to come; once the famine was underway,

Joseph would see how his hardships had been part of a providential plan to save his estranged family!

As bold as he was, Joseph was not prideful, but humble. Pride and arrogance had been stripped from him long ago. Now, he was a man graced with authentic humility. He embraced his God-given role without apology and honored his God-given gifts by offering them in service. The myriad elements of his life, many of which seemed mismatched before, now converged in perfect harmony with one another.

At this point of convergence there was an exchange of missing pieces. Pharaoh provided Joseph with the ultimate opportunity *and* got what he and his people needed. The Law of the Missing Piece was fulfilled. At this point of unfolding destiny, three essentials emerge:

Recognition—Pharaoh saw in Joseph extraordinary wisdom, integrity, and character. Therefore, he valued the plan Joseph proffered as a solution to the coming famine. Pharaoh's servants agreed that Joseph's proposal was good for Egypt.

> Now the proposal seemed good to Pharaoh and to all his servants. Then Pharaoh said to his servants, "Can we find a man like this, in whom is a divine spirit?" So Pharaoh said to Joseph, "Since God has informed you of all this, there is no one so discerning and wise as you are."[4]

What an outstanding turn of events! Minutes earlier, Joseph's life seemed to be at a standstill. Now, suddenly, he was on the ultimate fast track to destiny fulfillment!

Think It Through _____

Imagine yourself in a similar situation, because it is coming. If you will grasp your destiny codes, the day will come when the person who holds your missing piece will cross your path and see you for who you really are. Then he or she will say, "I need what you have. Nobody has what you have. You are *the one!*"

Activation—Pharaoh's recognition of Joseph made way for Joseph's specific assignment. Pharaoh appointed him to oversee the nation and direct Egypt's preparation for, and distribution during, the famine. Pharaoh made room at the top for Joseph and signified his activation in a very public and symbolic way:

> "You shall be over my house, and according to your command all my people shall do homage; only in the throne I will be greater than you." And Pharaoh said to Joseph, "See I have set you over all the land of Egypt." Then Pharaoh took off his signet ring from his hand, and put it on Joseph's hand, and clothed him in garments of fine linen, and put the gold necklace around his neck.[5]

Pharaoh activated Joseph's new role. He honored him and lavished upon him garments and jewels that identified him as a man of authority with the full backing of Pharaoh. With the endowment of these symbols, Joseph was inaugurated into his office. He was empowered to act in his ordained capacity to produce the results both he and Pharaoh desired. There would be no question—everyone in Egyptian society would recognize Joseph's position, purpose, and identity.

Acceleration—Pharaoh fully embraced Joseph's recommendations and recognized their urgency. He wasted no time in getting his right-hand man into the field of action:

> And [Pharaoh] had [Joseph] ride in his second chariot; and they proclaimed before him, "Bow the knee!" And he set him over all the land of Egypt. Moreover, Pharaoh said to Joseph, "Though I am Pharaoh, yet without your permission no one shall raise his hand or foot in all the land of Egypt."[6]

Joseph was the ancient equivalent of a jet-setting ruler. He traveled throughout Egypt gathering and storing food during the seven years of plenty so that there would be enough food for the people when the seven years of famine arrived.

Can you see how Joseph's defining moment ignited the balance of his destiny path? As he stood before Pharaoh, the convergence of all that Joseph had learned, become, and been prepared for over the course of his lifetime was revealed. In one incredible moment his natural abilities, skills, spiritual inclinations—plus the abilities developed and refined in prison and in Potiphar's house—coalesced into a perfectly formed gift cluster.

Have you ever thought, "I'm a jack of all trades and master of none?" It is time to rethink your assessment. Don't discard anything you have done or learned to do; all of it is valuable and marketable. Somebody needs all that you have. Your defining moment will come. Like Joseph, you have in your personal history all the resources you need to build the perfect platform for your destiny future!

The Rest of the Story

In Chapter 9, we talked about the context of your destiny, which is relationship. At the end of our discussion, I said that your destiny is not only about *your* destiny: it is about blazing a trail for others.

While it is true that provisions for your betterment and benefit are written into your destiny DNA, your destiny code does not exist for your benefit only.

The Creator has a more complex plan for you than that. You were created to be a benefit to others; therefore your destiny code contains provision for accomplishments that do more than feather your nest. You are here to flourish by meeting needs.

This is not a book about the ancient Hebrews—and if it were, it would take another volume to cover the effect of Joseph's life upon his own family and nation. Suffice to say that Joseph's destiny code was not violated when Joseph suffered betrayal by his brothers. As traumatic an experience as it was, his banishment to Egypt was the elegant solution to the devastation Joseph's family would face in the future!

The famine in Pharaoh's dream affected an entire region. Because of Joseph, Egyptians were the only ones who were prepared for famine. Although Joseph's family was prosperous, the drought would eventually have wiped them out. Instead, they must have learned that the Egyptians had food to spare, because Joseph's father sent his brothers to Egypt with enough money to buy food.

Although his brothers had brutalized him, Joseph had long ago forgiven them. How do we know this? It is evident in his behavior when they came to Egypt to buy food. They did not recognize their brother. He looked like an Egyptian. Being shepherds, they were despised in Egypt. Joseph could easily have refused their money and sent them home to die, much as they had done to him. Instead, after thirteen agonizing years, Joseph showed his brothers love and compassion.

There was no bitterness in Joseph's heart. By the time he was reunited with his brothers, he understood that his suffering had been, in large part, for their sakes. He treated them well and at the right time revealed his identity:

> Then Joseph said to his brothers, "I am Joseph! Is my father still alive?" But his brothers could not answer him, for they were dismayed at his presence. Then Joseph said to his brothers, "Please come closer to me." And they came closer. And he said, "I am your brother Joseph, whom you sold into Egypt. And now do not be grieved or angry with yourselves, because you sold me here; for God sent me before you to preserve life. For the famine has been in the land these two years, and there are still five years in which there will be neither plowing nor harvesting. And God sent me before you to preserve for you a remnant in the earth, and to keep you alive by a great deliverance. Now, therefore, it was not you who sent me here, but God; and He has made me a father to Pharaoh and lord of all his household and ruler over all the land of Egypt. Hurry and go up to my father, and say to him, 'Thus says your son Joseph,' "God has made me lord of all Egypt; come down to me, do not delay.'"[7]

Because Joseph was Pharaoh's second in command, the Hebrews were saved from the destruction that famine promised. And Joseph's father was spared the sorrow of going to his grave with his heart still broken for his lost son.

Able to provide, with Pharaoh's full support, all that his family needed, Joseph arranged for them to be reunited with him. What an exquisite example of the workings of destiny codes! What a glorious ending to what seemed to be a horrific life story!

On the day of his macro moment—a day that started out like any other day during his exile—Joseph entered the portal of destiny fulfillment and never looked back.

Your macro moment awaits *you*. Are you ready?

Download Your Code

1. Imagine that you are Joseph, exiled in a foreign land, imprisoned on false charges, and suddenly summoned from the pit for an audience with Pharaoh. Describe your feelings. How can you prepare now for your coming macro moment?
2. Describe the dream that is incubating in your life and heart. Do you believe that your missing piece could be revealed tomorrow? Why or why not? How does this belief affect your unfolding destiny?
3. Name the elements of your dream that are already coming together. How would their convergence in a defining moment change your life today?

Notes

1. The details of Joseph's story as noted in this chapter are taken from the Book of Genesis, chapters 37 and 39-47. All direct Bible quotes are documented individually.
2. Genesis 41:15 (New American Standard Bible).
3. Genesis 41:33-36 (New International Version).
4. Genesis 41:37-39 (New American Standard Bible).
5. Genesis 41:40-42 (New American Standard Bible).
6. Genesis 41:43-44 (New American Standard Bible).
7. Genesis 45:3-9 (New American Standard Bible).

Conclusion

You are reading this page. That says two things about you:
First, you have a sense of destiny. Second, it is important to you.
Yet, it says more; it tells me that you are finished with a wait-and-see
lifestyle. You want to live in The Zone—the tangible but not necessarily
physical place where the destiny engine fires on all cylinders and thrusts
you forward—not just anywhere, but to a place with your name on it.

—Mark Chironna, *Seven Secrets to Unfolding Destiny*

We started this journey together with the stone-cold statement that this world has been shaken to its core. You no longer need to pick up a newspaper to know this is true. But you also know that you were born with a code—a destiny code that reveals your magnificent purpose in life. That *knowing* cannot be dislodged from your heart. It is part of who you are. It explains life's symmetry and seeming contradictions. It reminds you that the world economic climate is not a contradiction of your destiny code; it is part of your destiny code. You *know* there is a place with your name on it. You might not have all the details worked out in your mind. You may not have picked out the drapes just yet, but you know it is still ahead.

The acknowledgment of your destiny is not delusional. Your destiny, which is your *identity,* is not an escape mechanism. Knowing your destiny code is not license to deny the shortfalls of your current circumstances. It means taking account of your situation, knowing that the comparison between where you are and where you are going is not a negative, but a yardstick. You read your progress and make adjustments every step of the way.

When life seems out of kilter, you process the pain and move forward. You know that the circumstances from which you long to be delivered are essential to your destiny training. They are reasons to keep pressing. They are symbols and signals of your destiny code, so you dig below the surface; you get past the noise; you unearth the meaning. Your perseverance pays off and produces an even clearer picture of your purpose.

On the road of destiny fulfillment you keep in front of you the reminders, not of what you have lost, but of all you are gaining. You imagine how your life of destiny fulfillment will feel, how it will taste, how it will smell, and how it will serve others. You handle the end result in your mind's eye so that your goals become laser-focused and your preparation continues. Like a wise master builder, you fashion each of life's supporting beams on the basis of the finished structure that is your destiny.

When you drill down into your destiny code, you see the finished product of your life's purpose even before you find the "forest" from which your supporting beams will be hewn. With the end result in mind, you choose the right lumber from the best sources. You will shape those beams with care, carving every detail with intentionality to support what does not yet exist: your future.

With every effort, you are building the structure that is *you*. Through good times and bad, through joys and sorrows, you are being seasoned and sculpted to become the full manifestation of the person you were born to be. The process is invigorating and excruciating. There will be highs and lows, sweet surprises and chilling upsets. Yet, even when you feel stuck at rock bottom, you have the presence of mind to know that every experience is a signpost pointing you toward the someplace that has your name on it.

Like Michael J. Fox, you will discover that your hardest days can be your best. Like Francisco Bucio, you will embrace unusual solutions that yield outstanding results. Like Joseph, you will discover that your "impossible" dream, the destiny that is so far out of reach, is actually closer than arm's length, because it is in your heart.

There *is* power in a story. The life of another human being reminds us that we are just like those who blazed their destiny trails before our eyes. But, as I have said from the start, this book is first and foremost about *your* story—your powerful, incredible, perhaps yet-to-be-celebrated story. Your capacity for destiny achievement is as great as or greater than even those whose stories we have honored!

Wherever life has taken you so far, however in or out of control you think you are, you have the power to live on the cutting edge of your possible reach. That cutting edge is the place beyond your comfort zone where your destiny pops. It is the place where destiny connections seem to materialize from thin air and invisible lines of supply become visible. It is the place of influence which you were created to occupy, the place of power and accomplishment for which you are currently being groomed. Above all, it is the place to which you are being sent to touch the lives of others in ways you have not yet dreamed possible.

Regardless of how you see yourself, whether strong or weak, rich or poor, able-bodied or challenged in some way, you have within you the power to live on that cutting edge. You are free to reject the dull edge of security for security's sake. You are equipped to assume some destiny risk. You are ready to affirm a life—*your* life—that is bigger and impactful and fulfilling, simply because you were willing to go there!

Each of us has been given the raw material of greatness: instincts about how things work, glimpses of giftedness, creativity and ingenuity, a desire to contribute to society, a hunger for something more, a thirst to excel and exceed our past efforts and even the accomplishments of others. The fact that you took the time to read this book speaks volumes; it tells me that you are ready to use your raw material; you are ready to unearth what has been buried under layers of fear, doubt, rejection, and self-protection. You are ready to throw off the weight of past failures and the even the dream killers whose taunts prove that you are onto something big.

You are ready to work with all that God gave you—and you will do it as if your life depended on it. You are ready to run with what have as though it were all you ever needed, knowing that new sources will open up each step of the way and facilitate every endeavor that is part of your glorious future. You have seen that there is a path out of every pit. You know by now that nothing is impossible unless you deem it so.

Even if you have been discouraged in the past, whether for days or decades, today is your day to come out of the pit, dust yourself off, and become somebody's solution. You may have lost your cutting edge more than once, but you know that is not the end of your story. You have identified self-sabotaging tendencies from times past, but you are facing them head on. You know how to let the right people come alongside you and help you to overcome the hindrances that used to impede your path.

You know the difference between recycling old trash and re-purposing past experiences for the sake of renewal. You recognize the patterns in your life; know how to process them without perpetuating them. You know now, like never before, that your future determines your present and your present is serving its purpose in the grand design of your life.

You know that somebody out there has your missing piece—and you know that he or she needs what you have in order to achieve *their* destiny fulfillment. You realize, probably with greater expectation and excitement than ever before, that your life can be transformed in an instant. A single defining moment can blow the boundaries off your life and cause you to be a benefactor, possibly to millions.

This is your invitation to mine the depths of your destiny code…to break through the limitations you thought were there to hem you in…and to press into the life you were created to live—the place where you find the full expression of the amazing person you already are and are yet to become.

Accept the invitation. It has your name on it.

CPSIA information can be obtained at www.ICGtesting.com
Printed in the USA
LVOW07s1206051013

355461LV00006B/12/P